Country
Inspirations

TRADITIONAL
COOKING

*A Guide to Delightful Home Style
Recipes & Gifts from Nature's Harvest*

SHOOTING STAR PRESS

This edition published in 1995 for:
Shooting Star Press, Inc.
230 Fifth Avenue, Suite 1212
New York, NY 10001

First published in 1992.

Publisher: Robin Burgess
Publishing Manager: Rachel Rush
Project coordinator: Lynn Bryan, The Bookmaker
Designed by Watermark Communications Group Ltd
Illustrator: Peter Byatt
Photographers: Ray Jarratt and Clive Streeter
Production team: Simon Rimmington and Alison Guthrie
Color separation: G. A. Graphics, Stamford
Printed in Singapore by Imago

Title: Traditional Cooking
ISBN: 1 57335 280 2

Country
Inspirations

TRADITIONAL
COOKING

A Guide to Delightful Home Style
Recipes & Gifts from Nature's Harvest

CONTENTS

Introduction

Making Jams & Marmalades

Making Chutneys & Pickles

Homemade Gifts

CONTENTS

Cooking
with Cheese

Soups &
Starters

Party Dishes

Introduction

Welcome to the wonderful tradition of home cooking in the country kitchen!

This book contains the quintessential traditional home-baked recipes our mothers used to make. Tried and tested, healthy and nutritious recipes to make your mouth water have been selected to bring you the ultimate country kitchen compendium.

Using fresh country produce is one of the most enjoyable ways to cook for family and friends. From the country pantry are recipes for making fruit jellies and marmalades and conserves; from the well-worn pages of mother's stained recipe book are delicious recipes for beet chutney, tomato chutney, honey dew melon pickle and spiced quinces. And many more accompanying delights.

Once you have mastered the above, move on to the chapter featuring homemade gifts, making country-style mustard, mint vinegar and genuine tomato sauce — to list but a few of these edible gifts.

In the 'Soups and Starters' chapter, more gourmet treats await the traditional cook. "Soup is to dinner what the porch or gateway is to a building," a famous French chef once wrote. It leads to the main course. Tempting summer starters like marinated mushrooms and roasted pepper salad will impress the guests. Vegetable soups, thick and steaming hot, accompanied by country-style breads, make the best meals for late fall and mid-winter luncheon parties. Remember to use what is in season. Be experimental and adventurous with your combinations.

Cooking with cheese brings a variety of recipes into your repertoire. Cheese can be used in soups, souffles and snacks, pizzas, pastry and in vegetable dishes — and desserts. Learn how to make your own fresh cottage cheese and cream cheese as well as water biscuits, bubble breads and olive bread to eat with your cheese.

Finally, the section on cooking for a party challenges you to use the skills learned throughout this book to create a memorable feast, whether it be for 10 or 50 people. From chili con carne for a teenage party to cold salmon trout for a more sophisticated gathering, many of the recipes have been chosen for their suitability to prepare in advance. The recipes are presented with simple straight-forward instructions. To help with organization, there are invaluable tips on preparing, storing and serving your party food.

It is very satisfying to serve and to eat something you have made yourself. What you have made will always be of a finer quality than anything you could buy, and you will have saved money. Look for the 'Cook's Notes in each chapter. Read the recipes carefully before preparing to cook and have everything you need ready at your fingertips. From this moment on you, too, can make country-style foods just like those mother made.

Making Jams
and
Marmalades

JAM & MARMALADE MAKING

These are old-fashioned marmalades made from seville oranges.

them all the year round. Jams, jellies, conserves and pastes can also be turned into a dessert or a sauce for a meat dish.

Throughout the recipes, different quantities of fruit are specified. Some are large amounts, for when there is a glut of that particular fruit. They will still work if you carefully halve the ingredients. Others are smaller and more manageable. Read 'Making Jam', before trying any of the recipes to avoid the dread of every jam maker — a failed set.

Scrub the skins of fruit thoroughly before using, in order to remove any pesticides and the wax used to make the skins shiny.

Whenever various fruits come into season, it is time to buy them in bulk and make the appropriate recipe.

The heaps of shining oranges, apples or plums immediately make one think of making orange marmalade, apple paste or plum and ginger jam. Preserve peaches and apricots and pears while they are cheap so that family and friends can enjoy

MAKING JAM

A good jam is bright and clear and tastes of the original fruit. It should be set but not solid, and of course it should keep well. Total success in all these respects may not always be possible, because the quality of the fruit varies according to its sugar and water content and ripeness. Over-ripe fruit tends to lose flavor and pectin, which is what helps the jam to set. Even the size and shape of the saucepan can affect the rate of evaporation of the water. If you follow the basic guidelines laid out in this introductory section, you should be able to avoid mishaps.

FRUIT
The fruit should be as fresh as possible and slightly under-ripe, as this is when pectin is at its highest. Pectin is a natural gum-like substance in some fruits; when boiled with sugar it forms into a jelly. The presence of acid is also essential. Acid helps extract the pectin, brightens the color, improves the taste, and helps prevent crystallization.

All fruits do not contain the same amount of pectin and acid. Pectin and acid are easily added to the low-pectin fruits in the form of citrus juice. You can also mix a fruit that is high in pectin, like apple, with one low in pectin, like blackberry. Commercial pectin is available, but I prefer lemon juice or to mix the fruits.

The fruit needs to become soft before the sugar is added. The process of softening breaks down the cell walls of the fruit and releases the pectin. Generally the fruit is brought gently to a boil and then allowed

to simmer from 30 to 60 minutes to soften the fruit. Sometimes extra water is added to prevent burning; the amount needed depends on the water content of the fruit and the quantity in the saucepan.

FRUITS HIGH IN PECTIN & ACID	FRUITS LOW IN PECTIN & ACID
Cooking Apples	Apricots
Crab-Apples	Peaches
Blackcurrants	Cherries
Redcurrants	Blackberries
Gooseberries	Raspberries
Grapes	Mulberries
Plums, Damsons	Strawberries
Quinces	Pineapples
Lemons, Limes	Pears
Grapefruit	Melons
Oranges	Passionfruit
Mandarins	Tomatoes
Cumquats	Marrows
Guavas	Rhubarb

SUGAR
Sugar is very important because it preserves the fruit and enables it to set. It also helps to retain the natural fruit flavor and color. Too little sugar will prevent the jam from setting; too much will darken and sweeten the jam.

Apricot jam made from dried apricots is delicious on homemade wholemeal bread fresh from the oven.

COOK'S NOTES
Standard spoon and cup measurements are used in all recipes.
All spoon measurements are level spoonfuls.

Use granulated, preserving or superfine sugar, as unrefined and raw sugars will smother the flavor of the fruit. Light corn syrup or honey will do this too.
Some recipes require the sugar to be warmed. To do this, put it in a baking dish, spread it out, and put the dish in a slow oven for 10 minutes. Warming enables the sugar to dissolve faster and is done when using fruits that need to be boiled for only a short time.
Try to avoid stirring the jam after the sugar has dissolved.
The golden rule for jam making is slow and long cooking to soften the fruit before adding the sugar, then very fast and short cooking as soon as the sugar has dissolved. Follow this advice for success.

THE SETTING POINT

The setting point is the exact time to finish the cooking. The jam will not set properly if it does not reach it, and if the cooking goes beyond this point, the jam will darken and crystallize. There are three ways to determine the setting point and these are as follows:

Saucer method

Take a small saucer cold from the freezer and drop some jam onto it. As the jam cools, it should set and crinkle if you push it with your finger. Turn the plate upside-down and if the jam still sticks, the setting point is reached.

Spoon method

Dip a wooden spoon into the jam, remove, and hold the spoon horizontally until the jam is slightly cooled. Turn the spoon gently; if the jam falls off in heavy flakes, it is at the setting point.

Temperature method

Use a sugar thermometer and when the jam reaches 221°F, the setting point is reached. (It is a good idea to invest in a quality sugar thermometer to ensure long-term accuracy.)

BOTTLING THE JAM

As soon as the setting point is reached, remove the saucepan from the heat and remove any scum that may have formed. Allow to stand for 10 to 15 minutes so the fruit distributes evenly through the jam, then pour the jam into clean jars that have been sterilized by heating in a slow oven for 30 minutes. Make sure there are no air bubbles in the jam; dispel any air bubbles with a spatula.

Air bubbles harbor bacteria. Fill the jars to the top, as the jam will shrink as it cools. Wipe the jars down; wipe inside the rim. Either seal straight away or cover and wait until the jam is completely cool.

Cover and seal with screw–top lids or cellophane. Moisten the cellophane when you put it on to ensure it is smooth and tight-fitting. Paraffin wax, obtainable from a pharmacy, makes an excellent seal.. Melt it over a low heat and pour just enough over the jam to seal it completely.. If you want to keep the jam a long time, this is the best seal. You can still put a pretty paper or cloth cover over the seal and tie it on with ribbon.

COOK'S NOTES
Some fruits can be frozen when brought if it is not possible to make jams and marmalades immediately.

Tomato jam , served with fresh bread and fresh fruit, is a delicious informal snack.

much faster that it is possible to be spontaneous making jams and to experiment with different blends of fruit.

MAKING CONSERVES
In making conserves, whole fruit or large pieces are preserved and set with pectin, acid and sugar as in jam. Conserves make a lovely dessert. Follow the instructions for making jam.

MAKING FRUIT JELLIES
A good fruit jelly is bright and clear and set but still a bit wobbly. The fruit taste should be noticeable. The same basic rules that apply to jam making apply here, with pectin, acid and sugar present in the right balance; but in making fruit jellies it is the strained juice from the cooked fruit that is boiled with the sugar to setting point. It is advisable to read 'Making Jam' before embarking on jellies.

FRUIT
The most suitable fruits are apples, crab-apples, currants, gooseberries and quinces, because they are high in acid and pectin. Other berry fruits and passionfruit are

EQUIPMENT
Use a large saucepan of stainless steel, enamel or aluminum. Never more than half-fill the saucepan, as the jam bubbles and spits near the setting point. Do not leave fruit longer than necessary in an aluminum pan. Use only a wooden spoon to stir the jam.

USING A MICROWAVE
Jams and marmalades can be made very quickly in a microwave oven. There are recipes on page 48. The fruit cooks so

delicious but not very high in pectin, so they are generally mixed with apple. The fruit should be fresh and just under-ripe. As the yield from the fruit is much less in jellies, it is best to make them out of windfalls or when fruits are cheaper.

Wash the fruit carefully; but as the pulp is going to be strained, do not concern yourself with removing stalks and cores and peel. The fruit is cooked in water first, the quantity depending on the water content of the fruit. Cooking is done slowly for about an hour until the fruit is very tender. In order to obtain a jelly, the fruit has to be broken down so that the acid and pectin are dissolved in the water.

STRAINING

The easiest method of straining is to use a jelly bag which will drip into a large bowl. They are not very expensive. The bag should be scalded before using. If you do not have a jelly bag, use a strainer lined with three layers of cheesecloth or a clean linen dish cloth and place the strainer over a large bowl. There is a third method: tie cheesecloth or a dish cloth to the legs of an upside-down stool so that when the fruit pulp is placed in the cloth it will drip into a bowl.

ADDING SUGAR

Measure the juice as you transfer it from the bowl to the saucepan. You will need exactly the same number of cups of sugar. The juice is slowly brought to a boil and then the sugar is added. Stir as the sugar dissolves. When it has dissolved, boil as rapidly as possible without stirring. It should take about 10 minutes to reach setting point. Use the same methods as for jam making to determine set.

BOTTLING

Take the saucepan from the heat as soon as the setting point is reached. Remove any scum from the surface with paper towels. Pour into warm sterilized jars immediately. Do not use large jars; small ones are best. Check for air bubbles; tilt gently to expel them. Seal while jelly is either hot or cold, not warm. Jam covers are fine for jellies. Paraffin wax is recommended for long storage. Do not move the jelly until it is completely cold or you may upset the jelling.

Label and write the date on the jars and then store in a cool, dry, dark place.

COOK'S NOTES:
Recycle all your old bottles and jars and soak off the labels or take them off with lighter fluid. You can cover up the screw-on lid with paper or cloth tied with a ribbon. Glue the cover onto the lid. Cellophane covers always look attractive. Dampen and put on hot jars to get a smooth effect. Try making your own covers, perhaps from muslin or a cross-stitch fabric.

COOK'S NOTES:
The pectin in citrus fruits is in the pith and seeds, so always keep them. Cook them in a cheesecloth bag with the fruit and take the bag out after the sugar has dissolved. Squeeze the bag thoroughly to extract the pectin, which should be allowed to drop back in with the fruit.

MAKING MARMALADE

Making marmalade is generally much easier than making jam because citrus fruits contain plenty of acid and pectin, so you do not usually have to worry about a good set. The golden rules for jam making apply equally to making marmalade, except that the thick peel of the citrus fruit takes longer to cook than the softer fruits of jam. Read the detailed instructions in 'Making Jam'.

The fruit should be as fresh as possible and slightly underripe; even the odd green one is fine. Scrub the skins hard to take off the wax that citrus fruit usually gets treated with to make it shiny.

To make jelly marmalade, fine shreds of peel without pith are needed. If you prefer chunky, thick marmalade, leave the pith on and cut coarsely. Always cut the fruit into the same-sized pieces for even cooking.

In citrus fruits the pectin is in the seeds and pith, so when making marmalade they are usually put in a cheesecloth bag to cook with the rest of the fruit. The bag is taken out just before the sugar is added and squeezed hard to extract all pectin, which is returned to the fruit mixture.

The fruit needs to cook for a long time, up to 2 or 3 hours, to soften the peel and extract the pectin. Sometimes extra lemon juice–that is, acid–is added to ensure a good set. As in jam, it is necessary to reach the setting point as quickly as possible after the sugar has dissolved.

Use the same setting point method as in jam making. Take the saucepan off the heat as soon as the setting point is reached. Remove scum. Allow to rest so the fruit distributes evenly through the marmalade. Pour into warm sterilized jars. Cover.

MAKING FRUIT PASTES, CHEESE & BUTTERS

Fruit paste and fruit cheese are used as a sweetmeat, served with cheese or instead of cheese. They are jelly-like but dense and have a beautiful color and delicate flavor. Serve them cut into wedges on a plate. Fruit butter is spiced and softer and does not keep very well unless sealed with wax. Serve as a spread for bread, scones and biscuits. Apples, quinces and damsons are the most common fruit used.

FRUIT PASTE & CHEESE

The fruit is washed, cut up, cooked just covered in water, and simmered until very soft, then puréed in a food processor. The pulp is measured by the cupful, and the same amount of sugar is added. It is stirred until the sugar has dissolved and gently simmered for about 45 to 60 minutes. It is ready when it is very thick and a wooden spoon can be drawn across the bottom of the saucepan without there being any running liquid.

Storing paste

The purée is poured into a shallow gratin dish not more than 1-inch thick. It now needs to dry out. In hot climates it can be dried in the sun, otherwise put into a preheated slow oven 300°F for about 20 to 30 minutes, then removed and allowed to cool. Either keep it in the dish and cut off the paste as required or turn it out and cut it into long bands and then into squares. Roll these in granulated sugar and wrap in waxed paper. Fruit paste does not need to be refrigerated. Keep it in a cool place.

Storing cheese

When the pulp reaches its required consistency, pour it into sterilized jars or molds, label and seal. Cover and label as for jams. Serve on a plate.

APPLE BUTTER

The fruit is simmered in the saucepan in vinegar and spices until the apples are soft and the vinegar has evaporated. The sugar is then added, and the mixture is boiled until thick. Store in sterilized jars with a wax cover if it is to be kept a long time.

COOK'S NOTES:
All equipment used in jam making should be scrupulously clean and dry. The bottles need to be sterilized and then filled either when warm or cold. Do not use tin, iron or copper spoons, skimmers or saucepan's for jams, as they can change the color and add an unpleasant flavor.

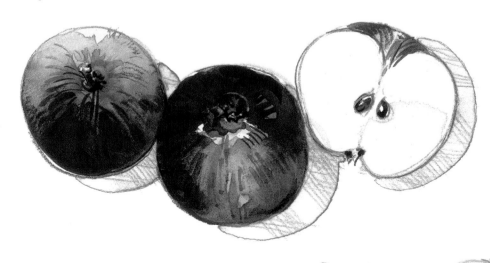

RECIPES FOR JAMS

APPLE & GINGER JAM

Ingredients
3 pounds cooking apples
2 cups water
Juice and peel of 2 lemons
1/2 teaspoon ground ginger
1/2 teaspoon ground cinnamon
3 pounds granulated sugar
4 tablespoons grated fresh ginger

Peel, core and dice the apples. The pectin in apple peel and cores is needed, so tie them up in a cheesecloth bag.

Put the diced apple, water, lemon juice and peel, ground ginger and cinnamon and the cheesecloth bag in a saucepan. Cook until the apple is tender. Add the sugar and grated ginger root, cook slowly until the sugar has dissolved. Squeeze the pectin out of the cheesecloth bag into the jam, then turn up the heat and boil very fast until the setting point is reached.

Remove the saucepan from the heat and let the jam stand for 10 minutes, then spoon it into sterilized jars. Label and seal.

DRIED APRICOT JAM

Ingredients

1 pound dried apricots
1 quart water
Juice and zest of 1 lemon
4 1/2 cups granulated sugar
1 cup slivered almonds

Soak the dried apricots in the water in a bowl. Leave for 12 hours, then transfer to a saucepan with the lemon. Bring to a boil, and simmer for about 40 minutes or until tender.

Add sugar and almonds; bring to a boil, stirring frequently. When the sugar has dissolved, turn up the heat and boil rapidly for 30 minutes or until the setting point is reached. Let the jam cool for 10 minutes, spoon it into sterilized jars, label and cover.

APPLE & BLACKBERRY JAM

Ingredients

2 pounds blackberries, hulled
1 1/2 cups water
12 ounces cooking apples,
*   peeled and thinly sliced*
3 pounds granulated sugar

Put the blackberries and half of the water in a saucepan and simmer until tender. At the same time put the apples and the rest of water into another saucepan and simmer until soft.

Now combine the blackberries and the apple along with the sugar, stirring until the sugar has dissolved. Keep the jam at a rolling boil until the setting point is reached.

Let the jam cool for 10 minutes, ladle jam into sterilized jars, label and cover.

Opposite page:
Use under-ripe Granny Smith apples for best results when making spicy apple and ginger jam.

APRICOT JAM

Ingredients

5 pounds apricots, halved and pitted
Juice and zest of 1 lemon
2 cups water
5 pounds superfine sugar

Put apricots, lemon and water in a saucepan and bring to a boil, stirring from time to time. Simmer until the apricots are tender. Then add the sugar and stir until it dissolves. Turn the heat up and boil rapidly for about 30 minutes or until the setting point is reached.

   Spoon the jam immediately into sterilized jars, label and cover.

BLACKBERRY JAM

Ingredients

Peel and seeds of 1 lemon
3 pounds blackberries, hulled
3 tablespoons water
2 tablespoons lemon juice
3 pounds granulated sugar

Tie lemon peel and seeds in a cheesecloth bag. Put it into a saucepan along with blackberries, water and lemon juice. Bring to a boil and simmer for 45 minutes or until berries are cooked. Add sugar, stirring frequently, and as soon as it dissolves take the cheesecloth bag out and squeeze the pectin out of it into the jam. Turn up heat and cook rapidly until the setting point is reached. Remove from heat and allow the jam to stand for 10 minutes, then spoon it into warm sterilized jars, label and cover.

CARROT JAM

Ingredients

1 pound carrots
Peel, seeds and juice of 2 lemons
2 tablespoons slivered almonds
2 cups granulated sugar
2 tablespoons brandy

Wash and scrape carrots and cut them roughly. You can chop them in a food processor, but not too finely. Put the lemon peel and seeds into a cheesecloth bag. Put the carrot pulp, lemon juice, cheesecloth bag, almonds and sugar into a saucepan and bring to a boil, stirring frequently. Take out cheesecloth bag, being sure to squeeze pectin out into jam. Keep up a boil until jam thickens, about 15 minutes. Take from heat and leave to cool for 20 minutes, then add brandy and mix well; this will act as a preservative. Spoon into sterilized jars, label and seal.

CHERRY JAM

Ingredients
3 pounds dark red cherries
Peel and seeds of 1 lemon
1 1/2 cups water
2 tablespoons lemon juice
2 pounds vanilla sugar

Remove pits from cherries and tie them up in a cheesecloth bag along with peel and seeds of the lemon. Put cherries into the saucepan with cheesecloth bag, water and lemon juice. Bring to a boil, stirring frequently. Simmer until cherries are tender, about 10 minutes. Add vanilla sugar. Once it has dissolved, remove the cheesecloth bag, squeeze out pectin, then boil rapidly until the setting point is reached. Leave jam for 10 minutes, then pot, label and seal.

Variation: A few of the cherry pits can be cracked, for the kernels will give the jam a bitter almond flavor.

FIG JAM

Ingredients
2 pounds fresh figs
Peel, seeds and juice of 1 lemon
1 cup water
1 pound granulated sugar

Take stalks off figs and any skin that comes off easily. Put lemon peel and seeds in a cheesecloth bag and place in a saucepan with figs, lemon juice and water. Slowly bring to a boil, stirring frequently. Simmer until figs are soft. Add sugar, and after it dissolves remove cheesecloth bag, squeezing the juice into the jam. Boil until the setting point is reached. Stir frequently, this jam tends to stick. Spoon into jars, label and store in a dark place.

DRIED FIG JAM

Ingredients
Peel, seeds and juice of 2 lemons
2 pounds dried figs, roughly chopped
2 quarts water
1 teaspoon fennel seeds
3 tablespoons pine nuts
1/2 cup slivered almonds
3 cups granulated sugar

Soak the dried figs in 4 cups of water for several hours. Put lemon peel and seeds into a cheesecloth bag. Place figs, remaining water, lemon juice and bag of peel and seeds in a saucepan and bring to a boil. Simmer until the figs are tender, stirring constantly.

Add fennel seed, pine nuts, slivered almonds and sugar, then stir until the sugar dissolves. Squeeze the juice out of the cheesecloth bag into the jam and discard. Boil, stirring constantly, until the setting point is reached. Ladle the jam into warm sterilized jars, cover and label.

GREEN GOOSEBERRY JAM

Ingredients
4 pounds gooseberries
3 cups water
4 pounds granulated sugar

Cut stalks and tails off the gooseberries. Put the fruit into a saucepan with the water and slowly bring to a boil. Simmer until the gooseberries are very tender, then add the sugar and stir until it dissolves. Bring to a rolling boil for about 15 to 20 minutes or until the setting point is reached.

Remove from the heat and let the jam stand for 15 minutes. Ladle it into sterilized jars, label and cover.

MELON & LEMON JAM

Ingredients
6 pounds sweet melon, peeled and diced
2 tablespoons grated ginger root
4 lemons, cut into thin slices
6 pounds granulated sugar

Boil the melon in a large saucepan until it is tender. Drain off water and add the ginger root and lemons. Bring to a boil, stirring constantly, and add the sugar. Stir until it boils. Boil for about 20 minutes or until it thickens and the setting point is reached.

Let it cool slightly before ladling it into warm, sterilized jars. Label and seal.

COOK'S NOTES:
Pectin, acid and sugar are necessary in the right proportions in order to get a jam to set well.

PEACH JAM

Ingredients
2 lemons
4 pounds peaches
4 pounds granulated sugar

Extract the juice from the lemons and put the chopped skins and seeds into a cheesecloth bag. Remove skin from the

peaches after pouring boiling water over them to facilitate skinning. Cut them in half and remove the pits.

Cook the peaches slowly in boiling water until they are tender. Pour off all the water. Add the lemon juice, sugar and a cheesecloth bag containing skins and seeds, and bring slowly to a boil; at this point remove the cheesecloth bag. When the syrup thickens and the peaches become transparent, the setting point should be reached.

Take the saucepan off the heat and let the jam stand for 10 minutes. Ladle into hot, sterilized jars, label and seal.

Pineapple jam is translucent and has a beautiful color and texture.

PINEAPPLE JAM

Ingredients
4 pounds chopped pineapple
Juice and zest of 2 lemons
3 cups water
4 pounds granulated sugar
1/4 teaspoon cayenne

Put the pineapple and lemon juice and zest into a saucepan with the water and bring to a boil. Simmer until the pineapple is tender, about an hour.

Add the sugar and cayenne, stirring constantly until the sugar has dissolved. Boil rapidly now for about 25 minutes or until the setting point is reached.

Take from the heat and leave for 10 minutes. Ladle into hot, sterilized jars, label and seal.

PEACH & PASSIONFRUIT JAM

Ingredients
10 passionfruit
4 pounds peaches
Juice and zest of 2 lemons
4 pounds granulated sugar

Extract the pulp from the passionfruit. Take the skins off the peaches after first immersing them in boiling water for several minutes.

Put the peaches into a saucepan and cover with the sugar, lemon juice and zest, and passionfruit. Slowly bring to a boil and then boil rapidly until the setting point is reached.

Take from the heat and leave for 10 minutes. Ladle into warm, sterilized jars, label and cover.

PLUM JAM

Ingredients
4 pounds plums
1 cup water
3 pounds granulated sugar

Remove the pits from the plums and put the fruit into a large saucepan with the water. Simmer until the plums are tender. Add the sugar and stir until it has dissolved. Boil rapidly for about 10 to 20 minutes until the setting point is reached.

Take from the heat and leave for 10 minutes. Ladle into jars, label and seal.

Variation: Add a tablespoon of grated ginger root when adding the sugar.

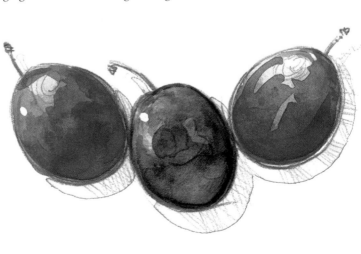

COOK'S NOTES:
The fruit is generally cooked slowly at first in water, the sugar being added at the end. The jam then cooks as fast as possible. This precaution will help prevent the jam from being spoiled.

PUMPKIN JAM

Ingredients
4 pounds pumpkin,
*   cut into 5/8-inch cubes*
2 lemons, sliced
1 quart water
4 pounds granulated sugar
2 tablespoons slivered almonds
1 teaspoon grated nutmeg

Make pumpkin jam in fall and winter when pumpkin is cheap and plentiful.

Slowly cook the pumpkin and lemons in the water until the pumpkin is tender. Add sugar, almonds, nutmeg and bring to a boil, stirring frequently. Boil until the syrup has thickened and the setting point is reached.

   Remove from the heat and let the jam rest for 10 minutes, then ladle into sterilized jars, label and cover.

REDCURRANT & ORANGE JAM

Ingredients
2 pounds redcurrants, stalked
2 oranges, finely sliced
2 pounds granulated sugar

Put the redcurrants and orange slices into a saucepan. Bring slowly to a boil and cook gently for 10 minutes. Add the warmed sugar and bring slowly to a boil again. Boil rapidly for 7 to 10 minutes or until the setting point is reached. Remove from the heat and let the jam stand for 15 minutes. Spoon into sterilized jars, label and seal.

RASPBERRY JAM

Ingredients
2 pounds raspberries, crushed
1 1/2 pounds granulated sugar

Combine raspberries and sugar in a saucepan and bring slowly to a boil, stirring constantly. The raspberry juice will soon begin to flow. When there is enough juice, boil rapidly until the jam is thick and the setting point is reached.

Allow to stand off the heat for 10 minutes, stir the jam once, then spoon it into sterilized jars, label and cover.

RHUBARB & GRAPEFRUIT JAM

Ingredients
2 grapefruit
2 pounds rhubarb, chopped
2 pounds granulated sugar

Take the zest off the grapefruit, then extract the juice. Tie the remaining pith in a cheesecloth bag. Combine all the grapefruit (including the bag of pith) and rhubarb with the sugar in a bowl and leave for an hour, transfer to a saucepan and bring to a boil, stirring frequently. When the sugar has dissolved, remove the cheesecloth bag, squeezing the pectin into the jam. Boil rapidly for about 15 minutes or until the setting point is reached.

Take the saucepan off the heat and let the jam stand for 10 minutes, then ladle into sterilized jars. Label and cover.

TOMATO JAM

Ingredients
6 pounds superfine sugar
6 pounds tomatoes
Juice and finely sliced peel of 2 lemons

Warm the sugar. Skin tomatoes, first pouring boiling water over them in a bowl to loosen the skins. Roughly chop them and place into a saucepan with the lemon juice and peel. Cook very slowly until the tomatoes are soft.

Add warmed sugar and stir until it has dissolved. Boil very fast for about 30 minutes or until it thickens and setting point is reached. It may take longer, as it depends on the water content of the tomatoes. Ladle into sterilized jars, label and cover.

COOK'S NOTES:
Always allow the jam to stand for 15 minutes after removing from the heat in order to allow the fruit to distribute evenly through the jam.

RHUBARB & ORANGE JAM

Ingredients
2 pounds rhubarb
3 cups granulated sugar
1 1/2 cups raisins
Juice and peel of 2 oranges
Juice and peel of 1 lemon

Wash the rhubarb and cut it into 8-inch lengths. Put it into a large saucepan, sprinkle the sugar over it, and add the raisins and the juice and grated peel of the oranges and lemon. Mix with a wooden spoon. Cover and allow to stand for 1 hour. Bring to a boil and cook slowly, stirring frequently, for about 30 minutes. Allow jam to cool slightly in the saucepan. Put into clean warm sterilized jars and cover at once. Label and date the jars.

STRAWBERRY & REDCURRANT JAM

Ingredients
3 pounds strawberries, hulled
1 1/2 pounds redcurrants, stalked
3 pounds granulated sugar

Put the strawberries and redcurrants into a saucepan and let them cook over a low heat. Meanwhile, warm the sugar in the oven. Keep stirring fruit as the juice starts running. When fruits are cooking in their own juice, add the warmed sugar and stir until sugar is dissolved.

Bring the jam to a rolling boil, stirring frequently until it thickens and reaches the setting point. It should take 15 to 20 minutes. Leave jam for 10 minutes off the heat before spooning it into sterilized jars. Label and seal.

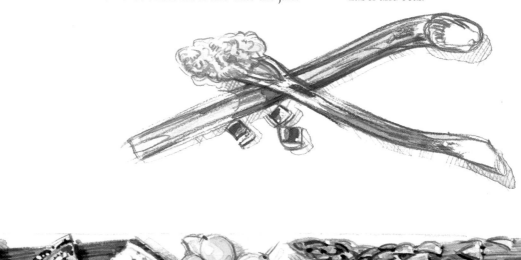

A perennial favorite, strawberry jam tastes delicious with warm croissants and coffee.

STRAWBERRY JAM

Ingredients
4 pounds granulated sugar
24 pounds strawberries, hulled
Juice and zest of 2 lemons

Warm sugar in a slow oven. Put the strawberries and lemon in a saucepan and heat gently, stirring as the juice begins to flow out of the fruit. While coming to a boil, add sugar. After it has dissolved, bring jam to a rapid boil until it thickens and reaches the setting point, about 15 to 20 minutes. Remove from heat and stand for 15 minutes. Ladle into jars, label and seal.

CONSERVES

CHERRY CONSERVE

Ingredients
4 pounds cherries
3 lemons
3 pounds 2 ounces granulated sugar

Remove the pits from the cherries. Slice the lemons finely and then cut each slice into halves. Place the cherries, sugar and half the lemons in a saucepan and leave for 12 hours. Put the saucepan on a low heat, add the zest of the lemons.

When it begins to boil, turn up the heat and boil rapidly until the setting point. Let the fruit stand for a while and then pour the warm conserve into sterilized jars. Label and seal.

STRAWBERRY CONSERVE

Ingredients
4 pounds strawberries
Juice and finely sliced peel of 2 lemons
4 pounds granulated sugar
1 teaspoon salt

Put the strawberries in a saucepan with the lemon juice and peel, and slowly heat, stirring constantly. The juice will soon sweat out of the strawberries.

When the fruit comes to a boil, add sugar and salt. Boil for about 15 to 20 minutes or until the setting point is reached.

Remove from heat and leave to stand for an hour, then pour into sterilized jars and cover and label.

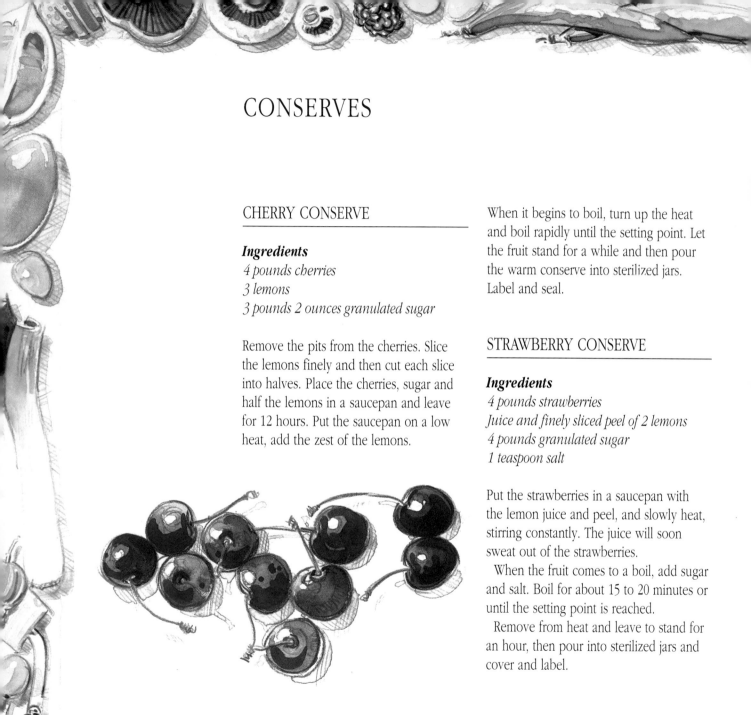

minutes, stirring constantly, for it will be sticky. When it reaches the setting point, remove from the stove and leave to stand for 15 minutes.

Pour the brandy into it and mix gently. Spoon into sterilized jars.

Eat this strawberry conserve with cream.

PEACH CONSERVE

Ingredients

4 pounds peaches
Juice and finely sliced peel of 2 lemons
3 pounds granulated sugar
2 tablespoons brandy

Skin the peaches, first pouring boiling water over them to make skinning easier. Halve and stone them and place them in a saucepan. Simmer gently in a tablespoon of water until the peaches soften.

Add the lemon juice and peel and the sugar and gently stir the mixture until the sugar has dissolved. Boil rapidly for about 10 minutes.

Remove from the heat. Leave for 30 minutes, stir in the brandy, then ladle into sterilized jars. Label and seal.

FIG CONSERVE

Ingredients

4 pounds figs
Juice and finely sliced peel of 2 oranges
Juice and finely sliced peel of 1 lemon
3 pounds granulated sugar
2 tablespoons brandy

Place the figs, orange and lemon juice and peel and sugar in a saucepan and slowly bring to a boil. Simmer for about 15 to 30

FRUIT JELLIES

COOK'S NOTES:
The fruit should always
simmer gently in water
and be very soft and
mushy before it is
strained. Never squeeze
the jelly bag if you want
a clear jelly.

APPLE JELLY

Ingredients
4 pounds apples or crab apples
Granulated sugar

Peel, core and chop the apples and put
them in a saucepan with just enough water
to cover them. Simmer for about an hour.
Strain the mixture through a jelly bag
hanging over a large bowl or through 3
layers of clean cheesecloth sitting over a
large saucepan. It will take 1 or 2 hours to
strain. Do not disturb the fruit or the jelly
will become cloudy.

Measure the juice; add 1 cup of sugar
each 1 cup of juice. Combine in a
saucepan and bring to a rapid boil.
Continue until the setting point is reached.

Remove from heat, skim, and pour
immediately into sterilized jars. Seal straight
away while the jelly is hot. Do not move
the jelly until it has finally set.

BLACKBERRY & APPLE JELLY

Ingredients
2 pounds blackberries
1 pound cooking apples
4 tablespoons lemon juice
2 cups water
Granulated sugar

Hull the blackberries; peel, core and chop
the apples. Put the fruit, lemon juice and
water into a saucepan and simmer until
tender.

Mash the fruit and strain it through a jelly
bag or layers of cheesecloth. It will take 1
or 2 hours to strain. Do not touch the jelly
bag. Measure the juice by the cupful, and
set aside the same amount of sugar. Bring
the juice to a boil and continue until it
thickens a little, then add the sugar. Stir
well and keep boiling rapidly until the
setting point is reached.

Immediately ladle into sterilized jars, seal
and label. Do not disturb jars until the jelly
is set.

APPLE & MINT JELLY

Ingredients
3 pounds green cooking apples
Juice and zest of 1 lemon
3 cups water
A bunch of fresh mint, washed and
*   roughly chopped*
1 cup white wine vinegar
Granulated sugar

Peel, core and chop the apples. Put them in a saucepan with the lemon and water, and cook slowly until the apples are tender. Add the mint and vinegar. Simmer for 10 minutes and then drain through a jelly bag. It will take 1 or 2 hours to strain. Do not squeeze the fruit juice.

Measure the liquid in cups and add the same amount of sugar. Bring to a boil and boil rapidly until the setting point is reached.

Remove from the heat and spoon into sterilized jars immediately. A sprig of mint can be put in each jar if liked, then label and seal.

MULBERRY JELLY

Ingredients
2 pounds mulberries
Juice and peel of 1 lemon
2 cups water
Granulated sugar

Remove the stalks from the mulberries and put the fruit into a saucepan with the lemon and water. Bring slowly to a boil and simmer for an hour or until the berries

Apple and mint jelly can be used as a sauce for meats as well as a spread for breads and cakes.

are very soft. Mash berries to extract all the juice. Strain through a jelly bag into a bowl. It will take 1 or 2 hours. Measure the juice. You need the equivalent amount of sugar. Put the juice into a saucepan and bring to a boil, simmer for 10 minutes, then add the sugar. Stir frequently until the sugar has dissolved. Bring the jelly to a rolling boil and continue until the setting point is reached. Pour immediately into sterilized jars, seal and then label.

PASSIONFRUIT JELLY

Ingredients
2 pounds passionfruit
2 lemons
5 cups water
Granulated sugar

Halve passionfruit and remove the pulp. Halve the lemons and extract the juice. Combine all the fruit (pulp, juice and skins) in a saucepan with the water. Bring slowly to a boil and simmer for about 30 minutes until the passionfruit skins are soft. Strain the mixture through a jelly bag. It will take 1 or 2 hours to strain. The next day, measure the liquid in cupfuls while

transferring it to the saucepan. You will need the equivalent amount of sugar. Bring fruit juice to a boil in a large saucepan, then add the sugar, stirring until it dissolves. Bring the syrup to a rolling boil and continue until the setting point is reached.

Ladle immediately into sterilized jars, label and seal. Do not disturb for a day or two until the jelly is set.

QUINCE JELLY

Ingredients
2 pound quinces
1 1/2 quarts water
Granulated sugar

Rub the furry down off the quinces and cut them up into smallish pieces. Put them into a saucepan with the water. Bring to a boil and simmer until the fruit is tender.

Strain the juice through a jelly bag into a bowl. It will take 1 or 2 hours. The next day, measure the amount of cups the juice makes, as you will need the same amount of sugar. Put the juice back into the saucepan and slowly bring to a boil. Stir in the sugar and keep stirring until it has dissolved. Bring the jelly to a rolling boil. Boil until the setting point is reached. Pour jelly into sterilized jars, label and seal.

Variation: Use apples, or crab-apples instead of quinces, following the same procedure.

REDCURRANT JELLY

Ingredients
3 pounds redcurrants, stalked
3 whole cloves
1 cinnamon stick
A piece of ginger root, bruised
3 cups water
1 cup white wine vinegar
6 cups granulated sugar

Put the currants and spices into a saucepan with the water, and simmer until the currants are soft. Strain the mixture through a jelly bag. It will take 1 or 2 hours.

Add the vinegar to the mixture and bring to a boil. Add the sugar, stirring until it dissolves, then boil rapidly until the setting point is reached – about 10 to 20 minutes.

Bottle in jars immediately, label and seal.

The taste and aroma of quince jelly are mouth-watering and well worth the effort involved in making this jelly.

MARMALADES

APPLE & GINGER MARMALADE

Ingredients
4 ounces ginger root
3 pounds cooking apples, chopped
1 1/2 quarts water
Juice and zest of 1 lemon
1 teaspoon ground cinnamon
3 cups granulated sugar

Cut ginger into julienne strips. Put it into a saucepan and cover with boiling water. Simmer for 20 minutes, then drain and refresh by placing under cold running water for 1 minute. Put the ginger in a bowl and cover with water. Leave in a cool place covered with a dish cloth for 2 hours.

Put the apples in the saucepan with the 6 cups of water and bring to a boil. Simmer for about 40 to 60 minutes until the apples are mushy. If you have a jelly bag, pour the apple into that with a bowl underneath to catch the juice. Otherwise put 3 layers of clean cheesecloth in a strainer which is set over a large bowl. Put the apple pulp into the cheesecloth and allow the juice to drip into the bowl. This will take 2 hours. Do not touch the fruit in any way or the jelly will cloud. Warm the sugar and measure the juice. If there is more than 4 1/2 cups of apple juice, put it in the saucepan and reduce to 4 1/2 cups. Now combine apple juice, lemon juice, zest, ginger and cinnamon in the saucepan. Gently heat, adding warm sugar; stir until the sugar has all dissolved. Bring to a boil and boil very fast for 15 to 20 minutes or until the setting point is reached.

Leave to stand for 15 minutes in a cool place. If there is any froth on the top, skim it off. Spoon into sterilized jars. Label, cover and seal when cold.
Leave for 2 weeks before opening.

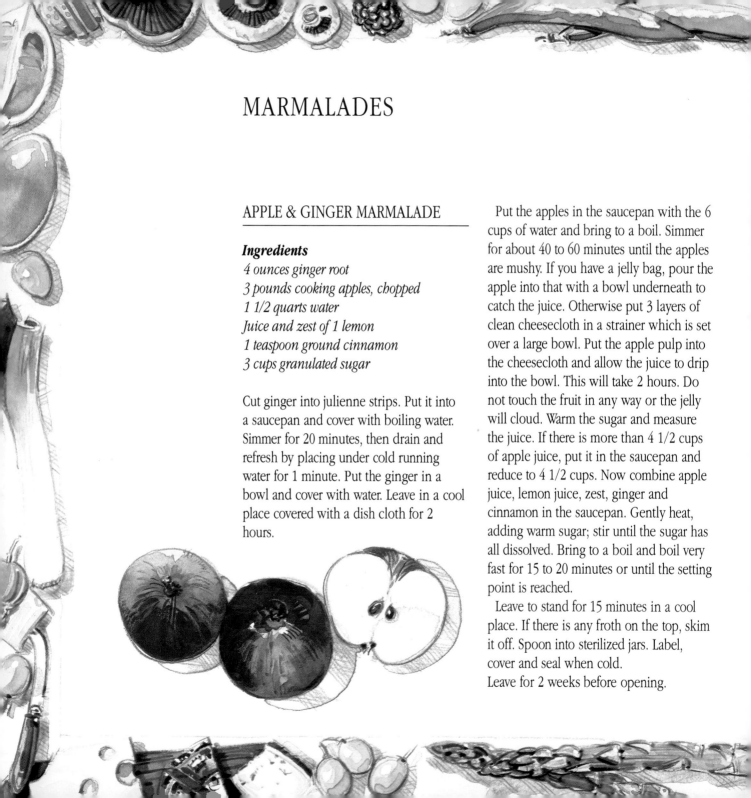

CUMQUAT MARMALADE

Ingredients

2 pounds cumquats
Juice and peel of 1 lemon
1 quart water
2 pounds granulated sugar

Slice the cumquats as finely as possible and remove the seeds. Put the seeds into a cheesecloth bag. Cut the lemon peel into fine julienne strips. Place the cumquats, lemon juice and peel and water in a saucepan with the bag of seeds and bring to a boil. Simmer for 1 1/2 hours or until the cumquat skins are tender. Take out the cheesecloth bag. Squeeze the bag thoroughly, allowing the remaining pectin to fall into the jam.

Add the sugar and stir until it dissolves. Bring to a rolling boil for about 25 minutes or until the setting point is reached.

Remove from the heat. Take off any scum and let the jam rest for 15 minutes before spooning it into sterilized jars. Cover immediately, label and seal when cold.

GINGER & ORANGE MARMALADE

Ingredients

3 pounds oranges
6 pounds muscovado sugar
4 tablespoons grated fresh ginger root
2 1/4 quarts water

Slice the oranges finely and put the seeds into a cheesecloth bag. Warm the sugar. Place the oranges, bag of seeds, ginger and

For those of you who do not like marmalade too sweet, try this cumquat marmalade.

water in a saucepan and bring gently to a boil. When the fruit is tender, add the sugar. Stir until the sugar has dissolved. Remove the cheesecloth bag and squeeze the pectin into the jam. Then boil rapidly for about 15 to 20 minutes or until the setting point is reached.

Remove from the heat and let it rest for 20 minutes. Remove any scum and spoon the marmalade into sterilized jars. Cover, label and seal when cold.

GRAPEFRUIT MARMALADE

Ingredients
2 grapefruit
3 lemons
2 pounds granulated sugar
1 1/2 quarts water

Cut grapefruit and lemons in half and squeeze out the juice. Strain the juice into a saucepan. Take some of the thick pith off

Grapefruit marmalade is made with slightly under-ripe fruit.

the grapefruit and put it, together with the seeds, in a cheesecloth bag. Slice the grapefruit and lemon skins.

Place them in the saucepan with the fruit juice; add the bag of pith and seeds and the water. Bring to a boil. When the peel is soft, add the sugar, stirring until dissolved. Remove the cheesecloth bag, squeezing out the pectin into the jam. Bring to a rolling boil and boil for 15 minutes or until the setting point.

Remove from the heat, take off any scum, and let the marmalade rest for 15 minutes. Pour into sterilized jars. Cover, label and then seal when cold.

MANDARIN MARMALADE

Ingredients
3 pounds mandarin oranges
1 lemon
2 1/4 quarts water
6 pounds granulated sugar
2 tablespoons whisky

Peel mandarins and cut the skin into julienne strips. Remove the seeds and put them into a cheesecloth bag. Chop the flesh. Take the peel off the lemon and cut

it into fine julienne strips. Strain the juice into a saucepan. Put the seeds and pith into the cheesecloth bag.

Place mandarin strips and flesh, the lemon strips and the bag of seeds and pith in the saucepan with the lemon juice and cover with the water. Bring to a boil slowly and simmer until the fruit is tender.

Add the sugar and stir until it has dissolved. Take out the cheesecloth bag, squeezing it hard to extract the pectin. Bring the mixture to a boil and boil rapidly until the setting point is reached.

Remove from the heat. Leave the marmalade to stand for 30 minutes, stir in the whisky and spoon into sterilized jars. Label and seal when cold.

LEMON MARMALADE

Ingredients
2 pounds lemons
4 pounds granulated sugar
3 quarts water

Take the peel off the lemons with a potato peeler. Cut it into julienne strips. Squeeze the juice out of the lemons and strain it into a saucepan. Save the seeds and the

COOK'S NOTES:
If the jam is overboiled, the sugar will darken the jam and may cause crystallization of the fruit and also spoil the taste. If the jam is 'runny', it could be due to under-boiling or a lack of pectin or acid, or too much sugar. Try to save it by reboiling with the juice and zest of 1 or 2 lemons.

pith and tie them in a cheesecloth bag. Place lemon peel, the bag of pith and seeds and the water in the saucepan with the juice and bring slowly to a boil. Simmer until the peel is tender, add the sugar, and stir until the sugar has dissolved. Remove the cheesecloth bag and squeeze it to extract the pectin. Bring to a boil and boil rapidly until setting point is reached. Remove from the heat and allow to cool down. Stir and spoon into sterilized jars.

LIME MARMALADE

Ingredients
2 pounds limes
1 1/2 quarts water
4 pounds granulated sugar

Slice limes as thinly as possible. Put the seeds in a cheesecloth bag. Place the lime slices, bag of seeds and water in a saucepan and bring slowly to a boil. Simmer until the lime slices are very tender.
   Add the sugar, stirring until dissolved. Remove the cheesecloth bag and squeeze the pectin into the jam. Bring to a boil and boil rapidly until setting point is reached. Remove from the heat and leave to stand

until it begins to cool. Stir the fruit once so that it is evenly distributed, and spoon the marmalade into sterilized jars. Seal.

OLD-FASHIONED MARMALADE

Ingredients
2 pounds Seville oranges
Juice of 1 lemon
2 quarts water
4 pounds granulated sugar

Cut oranges in half and squeeze out the juice. Strain it into a saucepan. Cut the peel finely, and put the seeds into a cheesecloth bag. Combine the juice and peel of the oranges with the lemon juice, the bag of seeds and the water in the saucepan. Bring slowly to a boil and simmer for up to 2 hours until the peel is tender. Add the sugar and stir until it has dissolved. Take out the cheesecloth bag and squeeze the pectin back into the marmalade. Bring to a boil and boil rapidly for about 10 minutes or until the setting point is reached.
   Remove from the heat, let the marmalade rest for 30 minutes, stir the fruit gently, and spoon into sterilized jars. Label and seal when cold.

This is a great, thick and chunky marmalade, perfect for breakfast on toast.

ORANGE MARMALADE

Ingredients
2 pounds oranges
1 lemon
4 pounds granulated sugar
2 1/2 quarts water

Cut oranges and lemon in half and squeeze out the juice. Keep the seeds and tie them up in a cheesecloth bag. Coarsely slice and chop the skins; do not take the pith off. Now put the orange and lemon skins, the juice, the bag of seeds and the water in a saucepan, bring slowly to a boil, and simmer for up to 2 hours until the skins are tender.

Add the sugar and stir until it dissolves. Extract the cheesecloth bag, squeezing the juice back into the jam. Bring to a boil, and boil rapidly for 15 to 20 minutes or until the setting point is reached.

Remove from the heat and leave the marmalade to settle for a while, then ladle into sterilized jars. Label and seal when cold.

and lime skins. Place them in a saucepan with the juice, pineapple, bag of seeds and the water. Slowly bring to a boil and simmer until the fruit is very tender.

Add the sugar and stir until it dissolves. Take out the cheesecloth bag and squeeze the pectin back into the jam. Bring to a rapid boil and cook fast until the setting point is reached. Remove from the heat and stand until it begins to cool. Stir once, then ladle into jars. Label and seal.

QUINCE MARMALADE

Ingredients
2 pounds quinces
2 quarts water
4 pounds granulated sugar

Peel and core the quinces and chop them into chunks. Put cores and peel into a cheesecloth bag. Place fruit, cheesecloth bag and water in a saucepan and slowly bring to a boil. Simmer for up to 1 1/2 hours or until the fruit is soft. Add the sugar, stirring until it has dissolved. Take out the cheesecloth bag and squeeze the pectin into the jam. Bring to a rolling boil until the setting point is reached.

COOK'S NOTES:
If you are planning on giving jam as a Christmas gift, decorate the jar with holly on the lid and red or green covers and ribbons. A red cover with a gold ribbon works well with a flower tied in with the ribbon. Put tartan covers on the jars with red ribbons and add a scroll of handmade paper with the recipe for the jam and serving suggestions.

PINEAPPLE, GRAPEFRUIT & LIME MARMALADE

Ingredients
1 pound pineapple
1 pound grapefruit
1 pound limes
2 1/4 quarts water
6 pounds granulated sugar

Peel, core and cut pineapple into small chunks. Cut grapefruit and limes in half, squeeze the juice and put the seeds into a cheesecloth bag. Finely slice the grapefruit

Remove from the heat. Take off any scum that has risen to the surface. Let the marmalade stand for 20 minutes, then ladle it into jars. Cover and seal when cold.

THREE-FRUIT MARMALADE

Ingredients
1 pound oranges
1 pound lemons
1 pound grapefruit
2 1/4 quarts water
6 pounds granulated sugar

Slice oranges and lemons finely and put the seeds into a cheesecloth bag. Remove the peel from the grapefruit with a potato peeler and cut into julienne strips. Add grapefruit pith and seeds to the cheesecloth bag. Squeeze out the grapefruit juice.

   Place slices of orange and lemon, the grapefruit peel and juice, the bag of seeds and pith and the water in a saucepan. Bring slowly to a boil and simmer for about 1 1/2 hours until the peel is tender.

   Add the sugar and stir until it has dissolved. Take out the cheesecloth bag; squeeze it to allow pectin to return to the jam. Bring to a rolling boil and cook until the setting point is reached.

   Remove from the heat and let it stand for about 15 minutes to distribute the peel evenly. Ladle into jars, label and seal.

A classic, this three-fruit marmalade is served with corn bread and lemon tea.

FRUIT PASTE, FRUIT BUTTER & FRUIT CHEESE

APPLE PASTE

Ingredients
2 pounds tart cooking apples
Juice of 1 lemon
1 1/2 pounds superfine sugar
A few drops of Angostura Bitters

Peel and core the apples and chop roughly. Put them in a saucepan with the lemon juice and enough water to cover them. Bring to a boil and continue to boil rapidly until the apples are very soft and translucent and the water evaporated.

  Put pulp through a food processor. Measure the pulp in cupfuls and add 1 cup of superfine sugar for each cup of pulp. Stir them together and leave for 2 hours, then put the apple and sugar mixture into a saucepan and boil until it has become very thick, stirring constantly. Add the Angostura Bitters, stir, then pour into a shallow ovenproof dish. It should be about 1-inch deep.

  The paste has to dry out slowly. Place in a slow oven 300°F for about 30 minutes, covered. When cool, cut the paste into squares and wrap in waxed paper. Store in a cool place.

APPLE BUTTER

Ingredients
2 pounds green cooking apples
Juice of 1 lemon
2 cups white wine vinegar
1 cinnamon stick
3 whole cloves
A piece of ginger root
1 pound granulated sugar
2 tablespoons rum

Peel, core and chop the apples and place them in a saucepan with the lemon juice, vinegar, and the spices wrapped in a cheesecloth bag. Bring to a boil and cook until the apples are soft and mushy and the vinegar has evaporated.

  Add sugar and stir until it has dissolved. Boil until it is a very thick mixture. Stir in the rum. Pour into jars, label and seal.

HARROSET

Ingredients

1/2 pound dates, pitted and
finely chopped
1/2 pound raisins, finely chopped
1 cup water
1 apple, grated
1 teaspoon ground allspice
1 teaspoon ground ginger
2 tablespoons chopped walnuts
1 cup granulated sugar

Soak dates and raisins in water for 12 hours. Put mixture in a saucepan and bring to a boil slowly. Add apple, allspice, ginger, walnuts and sugar. Stir constantly, as it is thick and sticky and will easily burn. When it is a thick paste, pour into an shallow china dish and allow to cool. Keep stored in a covered dish in a cool place.

RASPBERRY & APPLE CHEESE

Ingredients

2 pounds cooking apples
2 pounds raspberries
Juice of 1 lemon
Superfine sugar

Peel and slice the apples; hull the raspberries. Cook apples in enough water to cover them until they are soft and the water has evaporated.

Add raspberries and lemon juice then cook to a pulp. Purée fruit through a food processor. Measure the amount of pulp in cupfuls; for each cup of pulp you need 1 cup of sugar.

Put the fruit and sugar in the saucepan and cook, stirring until the sugar has dissolved. Bring to a rolling boil and continue until it is thick and a wooden spoon can cut across the mixture smoothly.

Pour into sterilized jars, label and seal.

PLUM GUMBO

Ingredients
2 pounds plums
A piece of fresh ginger root
1 cinnamon stick
4 whole cloves
1 cup water
2 cups golden raisins
2 oranges, thinly sliced
2 pounds granulated sugar

Remove the pits from the plums, then roughly chop the flesh and put it in a saucepan with the spices, tied up in cheesecloth bag, and the water. Bring to a boil and simmer until the plums are soft and the water has evaporated. Take out the cheesecloth bag.

Put plum pulp through a food processor and return it to the saucepan. Add the golden raisins, orange slices and sugar, bring to a boil and cook, stirring frequently, until the mixture is dark and thick and no running liquid remains. Put into sterilized jars, label and seal.

QUINCE PASTE

Ingredients
2 pounds quinces
1 1/2 pounds superfine sugar
Granulated sugar

Peel and core quinces, cut them into medium-sized pieces and put them into a saucepan with just enough water to cover them. Bring to a boil and simmer until the quince pieces are soft and water has evaporated. Put them through a food processor. Measure the pulp by the cupful, and for every cup of pulp add 1 cup of sugar. Put it all in the saucepan and bring to a boil, stir frequently until the mixture is thick.

Pour the paste into a shallow ovenproof dish and dry out in a slow oven 300°F. When cool, cut into squares and wrap in waxed paper. Store in a cool place.

Variation: After the paste has dried, spread a layer of slivered almonds between 2 layers of the paste.

PEACH PASTE

Ingredients
2 pounds peaches
Juice of 1 lemon
1 1/2 pounds superfine sugar
Granulated sugar

Pour boiling water over the peaches and soak in a bowl for a minute until the skins come off easily. Cut the peaches in half and remove the pits.

Chop the peaches roughly and put them into a large saucepan with the lemon juice and sufficient water to cover. Bring to a boil slowly and then simmer until they are tender.

Add the superfine sugar and stir until it has dissolved. Bring to a boil and cook rapidly until you have a thick paste. Put the paste into flat ovenproof dishes and dry in a warm oven.

Cut into squares, sprinkle with granulated sugar and wrap in waxed paper.

MICROWAVE JAMS

STRAWBERRY JAM

Ingredients
1 pound strawberries, hulled
1 tablespoon lemon juice
1 1/2 cups granulated sugar

Place strawberries and lemon juice in a large bowl, at least 12-cup capacity. Cover and cook on high for 5 to 6 minutes, until soft. Add the sugar and stir gently until dissolved. Cook on high, uncovered, for 12 to 15 minutes, until the setting point is reached; test for setting point frequently after 10 minutes.

Leave to cool slightly, then stir and pour into warm sterilized jars. Cover, seal and then label.

ORANGE & RHUBARB JAM

Ingredients
3 pounds rhubarb
Grated peel and juice of 1 orange
2 pounds granulated sugar

Wash rhubarb, trim well and slice across finely. Place in a large microwave cooking bowl with the orange peel and juice. Cover and cook in the microwave oven for 16 to 20 minutes on high, until very soft.

Add sugar, remove the cover from the bowl, and continue to cook on high for 20 minutes, until the setting point is reached. Cool slightly, ladle into hot sterilized jars, seal and label.

THREE-FRUIT MARMALADE

Ingredients
2 grapefruit
2 oranges
2 lemons
1 quart boiling water
4 pounds granulated sugar

Cut all fruit in half, squeeze the juice and set it aside. Remove the seeds and white pith from the peels and tie in a piece of cheesecloth. Slice the peel finely. Place the juice, peel and cheesecloth bag in a large

This orange and rhubarb jam is an interesting combination of flavors.

bowl and add 1 1/4 cups of the water. Leave to stand overnight.

Remove the cheesecloth bag and add the remaining boiling water. Cover and cook on high for 20 minutes, or until the peel is soft. Add the sugar and stir until dissolved. Cook, uncovered, on high for 25 to 35 minutes or until the setting point is reached; stir every 5 minutes and test for setting frequently after 20 minutes.

Leave to stand for 15 to 20 minutes to cool slightly, then stir and pour into sterilized warmed jars. Cover, seal and then label.

MAKING CHUTNEYS
AND
PICKLES

MAKING CHUTNEYS AND PICKLES

Made from summer fruits and vegetables and served with ham, roast meat and curried dishes, chutneys and pickles are among the easiest things to cook and they have the advantage of lasting for months or even years stored in a dark, dry closet. It is always such a pleasure in the middle of winter to open up last summer's pear pickle and enjoy the fruit of your labor. The opened jars also impart perfumes evocative of Asia, the Arab world and the Mediterranean region, the areas where many of the herbs and spices originated.

Use a fermented white wine vinegar. However, a quality malt vinegar is also perfect for rhubarb and date chutney. Cider vinegar is excellent.

Fruit and vegetables are available in a great variety these days. Even during hard times there is usually some item in abundance and cheap enough to buy in a large quantity. By preserving these things you can enjoy them at any time of the year. Chutneys and pickles are very good stand-bys for a quickly prepared meal or when visitors pop in unexpectedly. Most of the recipes in this chapter are for large quantities. You will find half quantities work just as well.

Fresh herbs are used unless otherwise stated. If they are unavailable, use half the quantity of dried herbs. Use freshly ground black pepper whenever pepper is used; add salt and pepper to taste.

INGREDIENTS

Apples, plums, red and green tomatoes, beets, dates, mangoes and rhubarb are the fruits and vegetables commonly used for making chutney. To these are added garlic, onions, chilies, spices, salt, sugar, and vinegar, the last three ingredients being the preservatives. The spices can be tied together in a cheesecloth bag and removed before bottling, but it is preferable to keep them loose in the chutney.

Use a fermented white wine vinegar. However, a quality malt vinegar is also perfect for such as rhubarb and date chutney. Cider vinegar is excellent.

Use coarse cooking salt, not the free-flowing salt that is placed on the table. Sugar helps to retain the fruit flavor as well as preserve the fruit. In these recipes you will find muscovado sugar or granulated sugar. Muscovado gives a darker color and taste. Superfine sugar is just as good. You can reduce the amount of sugar used by adding more dried fruits, such as dates, raisins or golden raisins, light corn syrup, molasses or honey. They will alter the taste, though, so be careful not to lose the taste of the original fruit as this flavor is the secret of success.

Hot chilies need careful handling. Be sure not to get seeds under your fingernails or to wipe your eyes while handling chilies. If you are not experienced, wear fine rubber gloves. Chili powder can be substituted, but use only a small amount. Chili sharpens the flavor of any dish wonderfully, but care should be taken not to use too much.

Garlic is one of the most valuable medicinal herbs. It improves the taste of any savory dish. Always use the fresh cloves. Throw away the garlic powder. Always use fresh ginger root. If you do not

have a supplier, substitute ground ginger, using half the amount required. Preserved ginger can also be used, but remember it will add more sugar to the recipe. Ginger adds a sharp tang to chutneys or pickles.

Other commonly used spices in chutneys and pickles are listed below in alphabetical order. They can be used whole, crushed or ground. I grind my own in a food mill, as they taste and smell so much better freshly ground. A coffee mill will grind them satisfactorily, but you should take care in cleaning the mill before and after use, to avoid transferring flavors.

Allspice has the aroma and taste of cinnamon, cloves and nutmeg, hence its name. The berries from the Pimenta dioica tree are used whole, crushed or ground.

Caraway seeds have a very distinctive aromatic taste. They are also excellent for the digestion. Pickles — and, of course, sauerkraut — are especially enhanced by caraway seeds.

Cayenne is finely ground dried red chili pepper. It also has digestive properties. It is very hot and adds an extra depth to the flavor of chutneys or pickles.

Celery seeds are used often in pickles and chutney. They have an excellent taste and are believed to help rheumatism.

Cinnamon comes from the bark of the tree *Cinnamomum zeylanicum*. It can be used in stick form or ground. Cinnamon has preservative and medicinal qualities and sharpens the flavor of pickles.

Cloves are a powerful antiseptic and add a pungent flavor to dishes. They are used whole or ground.

Coriander seeds have a pleasing spicy flavor. They can be used whole, crushed or ground in chutneys and pickles.

Fennel seeds are another spice with a very distinctive aromatic taste, as well as being reputed to have many medicinal properties.

Juniper berries give a delicious taste and aroma to food. They are also a digestive and are said to be good for the kidneys. Use whole or crushed.

Mustard seeds are best used whole in chutneys and pickles. They add a pleasant tang to many dishes.

Nutmeg is also a digestive and richly enhances any vegetable or fruit pickle. Freshly grated nutmeg from the large seed is far and away superior to the packaged already ground nutmeg.

Paprika is dried and ground from a red sweet capsicum (pepper). It is excellent as a flavoring or a garnish, adding its rich red color to the chutney.

Pepper is the king of spices. Always use black pepper for chutneys and pickles. Use whole or freshly ground.

Turmeric is ground from a dried aromatic root *Curcuma longa*. It is a brilliant yellow and adds fragrance and color to pickles and chutneys.

COOKING & BOTTLING CHUTNEY

Chutneys generally simmer for up to 2 hours, the fruit absorbing the vinegar during this time. When you can draw a wooden spoon across the bottom of the saucepan and there is no runny liquid left, the chutney is ready. As you become familiar with chutney making, you will recognize the sticky thickness that means the chutney is ready for bottling.

It is difficult to give an exact cooking time because the quality of fruit varies. As fruit gets older, it has less ability to absorb sugar. With the exception of red tomatoes, which should be ripe, buy fruit that is slightly under-ripe and firm.

It is the long cooking of the sugar which darkens the chutney. If you want a lighter chutney, add white sugar after the fruit has cooked pretty well.

Spiced quinces are a tasty addition to a picnic lunch. Try them with mild-tasting foods.

Only heavy-based enamel, or stainless steel saucepans should be used for cooking chutneys. Use a clean wooden spoon for stirring. Stir occasionally throughout the cooking time, especially towards the end when the chutney is thickening up. It is unwise to leave chutney unattended towards the end of cooking time.

Chutneys should be stored in glass jars. I save all the commercial jars and take the labels off by soaking them or removing the stubborn ones with lighter fluid or eucalyptus oil. Many of the jars are lovely

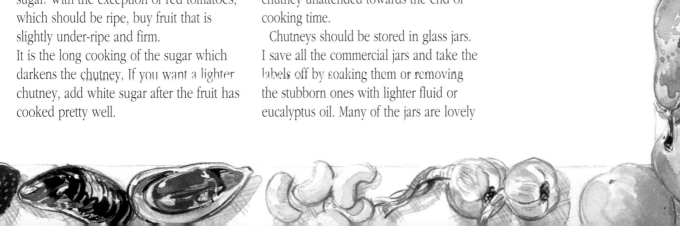

shapes. Bottle chutney while it is hot in clean jars. Sterilize jars by placing them in a low oven for 30 minutes.

Cover the chutney immediately after putting it into the jars. Chutney reduces in volume if it is not sealed with a dark, efficient seal. Plastic lids are fine, but do not use metal lids unless they have a plastic lining, as the vinegar will eat into the metal and cause spoilage.

Paraffin wax is excellent if you do not have a lid. You can buy it at a pharmacy. Melt it in a small saucepan and pour it over the chutney. You need enough to cover and seal the entire surface.

Make sure the jars are clean outside and inside between the chutney and the top of the jar. Another important thing to remember when bottling is to pack the chutney in so there are no air bubbles. Use a spatula to get rid of them; they are breeding grounds for bacteria.

Do not forget to label and date jars of chutney. Having gone to the trouble of making the chutney, it is a shame to waste the effort through not knowing what is in the jar and whether it is still good to eat. Chutney is best stored for 2 months before opening. Most chutneys will last up to 2 years. Once a jar is opened, refrigerate.

MICROWAVE COOKING

Chutneys can be made very quickly in the microwave. Some recipes are included on page 72. The general rule to convert the other chutney recipes for microwave cooking is to put all the ingredients into a large suitable bowl, cover and cook on the highest setting for 30 to 45 minutes or until thickened. Stir every 10 minutes. Watch very carefully in the last 15 minutes of cooking as it begins to thicken. Do not cook very large quantities of fruit and vegetables. The recipes can be reliably halved if you want smaller amounts.

FRESH CHUTNEYS

Fresh chutneys can be made just a few hours before they are to be eaten. They generally accompany a curry dish and cool the palate after the spiciness of chili dishes. Some are excellent as salads or for dipping with vegetables and bread. They are good to serve when you are waiting for the steak to cook on the barbecue.

Always use a skim-milk yogurt to make them. There are excellent yogurts available now in conveniently sized containers. Always whisk the yogurt smooth before adding the other ingredients.

These fresh chutneys can be fun to experiment with by changing the spices and the herbs and vegetables.

PICKLES

Fruit and vegetables are preserved, or pickled, by gently cooking in a sweet spiced vinegar. Again, salt, sugar and vinegar are the preservatives.

The vegetables and fruit should be fresh and almost ripe, with no blemishes. Pickles should always be stored in sterilized jars to within 1 inch of the top. The brine should cover all the fruit or vegetables. Check for air bubbles and dispel them, then seal the jars immediately. Metal lids should not be used unless lined with plastic, but glass lids are suitable. For further details, see the information on cooking and bottling chutney.

COVERING THE JARS

Make brown paper or fabric covers for the jars and glue them onto the lid. You can trace a circle onto your material from a saucer. After you glue it on, tie a ribbon or even kitchen string around it. Have a selection of labels ready. Try making your own; a tartan theme or a small floral print fabric makes attractive covers, especially when tied with matching ribbons. Black tissue paper with gold ribbon looks very dramatic. For Christmas, try using a handmade red paper, green ribbon and a sprig of holly.

This is where your creativity can be imaginatively used — and that of your family, too. Older children may like to help you make labels, or the covers.

The pumpkins and the beautiful red tomatoes are a delicious mixture in this chutney.

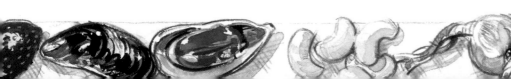

RECIPES FOR CHUTNEYS

Combine all the ingredients and bring to a boil. Simmer until the mixture thickens and ladle into sterilized jars. Seal straight away, label, and then store for 3 months before opening.

APPLE & PLUM CHUTNEY

Ingredients
1 cup sugar
1 teaspoon salt
1 teaspoon ground cinnamon
2 cloves
1 chili
2 cups white wine vinegar
5 cooking apples, peeled and chopped
10 plums, pitted and chopped
2 onions, chopped
1/3 cup fresh ginger, chopped
1/2 cup golden raisins

Put the sugar, salt and spices into a saucepan with the vinegar and bring to a boil. Add the apples, plums, onions, ginger and golden raisins, then simmer gently for

Use Granny Smiths for making this apple chutney. You will find the result more tangy.

APPLE CHUTNEY

Ingredients
3 pounds cooking apples, finely chopped
1 pound onions, finely chopped
1 1/2 cups sugar
1/2 cup water
2 tablespoons chopped ginger root
1 teaspoon ground cinnamon
3 red chilies
1/2 tablespoon salt
1 1/2 cups vinegar

about 1 1/2 hours until it is thick but still a bit runny. Put the chutney into hot sterilized jars, seal and label.

APPLE & TOMATO CHUTNEY

Ingredients

1 1/2 cups sugar
1 1/2 cups white vinegar
1 teaspoon ground ginger
1 teaspoon ground allspice
1 teaspoon ground black pepper
1 chili
1 teaspoon salt
6 medium tomatoes, skinned and chopped
3 cooking apples, peeled and chopped
1 onion, chopped
4 cloves garlic, chopped
1/2 cup golden raisins
1/2 cup prunes, chopped

Put the sugar, vinegar and spices into a saucepan and bring to a boil. Add the rest of the ingredients and simmer slowly for about 1 1/4 hours or until the mixture begins to thicken. Ladle into hot sterilized jars and cover.

APRICOT & DATE CHUTNEY

Ingredients

1 pound dried apricots, roughly chopped
1 1/2 cups golden raisins
1 1/2 cups white wine vinegar
3/4 cup brown sugar
1/2 pound dates chopped
1 1/2 tablespoons preserved stem ginger,
    chopped
1 cup water
1 tablespoon salt
1 1/2 teaspoons mustard seeds
1/2 teaspoon chili powder

Cover the apricots with water and leave to soak for 1 hour; drain. Place in a saucepan with the golden raisins and vinegar, bring slowly to a boil, and simmer for 15 minutes. Stir in the remaining ingredients, and simmer until thickened. Pour into hot sterilized jars, seal and label.

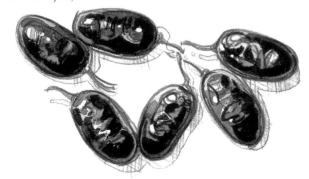

COOK'S NOTES:
Scrub or gently wash all the fruit and vegetables before cooking.

and simmer until thickened. Pour into hot sterilized jars, seal and label.

APRICOT & ORANGE CHUTNEY

Ingredients
1 pound dried apricots
4 oranges
2 onions, thinly sliced
3 cloves garlic, crushed and chopped
1 tablespoon allspice berries, bruised
2 tablespoons coriander seeds, crushed
2 tablespoons brown mustard seeds
2 cloves
1 cup golden raisins
1 pound sugar
2 tablespoons chopped ginger root
1 tablespoon salt
4 1/2 cups white wine vinegar

Soak the apricots for 1 hour; drain. Boil the oranges for 5 minutes, thinly pare the skin, and cut into thin strips. Remove the pith and chop the pulp. Tie up the allspice, coriander, mustard seeds and cloves in a cheesecloth bag.

Put all the ingredients into a saucepan, bring to a boil, and then simmer for about 1 1/2 hours or until the mixture thickens. Remove the cheesecloth bag and spoon

the chutney into sterilized jars. Seal and label immediately.

BEET CHUTNEY

Ingredients
2 pounds cooked beets
1 pound onions
2 cups sugar
1 teaspoon allspice berries, crushed
1 teaspoon mustard seeds
1 teaspoon coriander seeds
5 peppercorns
1 tablespoon salt
2 cups vinegar
1/2 cup flour

To cook the beets, cut off all except 2 inches of the tops, place the beets in a large saucepan, cover with water and simmer until tender. Remove skins when cool. Finely chop the beets and onions. This can be done in a food processor in several lots; use the pulse action, as the vegetables must not be reduced to a purée, just finely chopped.

Combine the beets and onion with the sugar, allspice, mustard seeds, coriander seeds, peppercorns, salt and enough vinegar to cover. Bring to a boil, and gently cook for about 25 minutes. Mix the flour to a smooth paste with cold water. Add to the beets, stirring to thicken, and boil for approximately 5 minutes more.

Pack the chutney into clean, hot jars when cool. Cover and label.

BENGAL CHUTNEY

Ingredients
6 apples, peeled and chopped
6 tomatoes, skinned and chopped
2 onions, chopped
3 1/2 cups brown malt vinegar
1 cup raisins
3 cloves garlic, finely chopped
3 fresh chilies
1 tablespoon mustard seeds
1/2 cup ginger root grated
1 tablespoon salt
1 1/4 cups sugar

Combine the apples, tomatoes, onions and vinegar in the saucepan. Simmer for about 15 minutes or until the onions and apples are soft. Cool, then add the remaining ingredients. Simmer until it is thick and sticky, about 45 minutes. Ladle into hot sterilized jars, then seal and label. This chutney improves with ageing. Keep for 3 months before opening.

Beet chutney is a great sanwich filler.

COOK'S NOTES:
Honey, light corn syrup or molasses can be used instead of sugar, but they have such distinctive flavors that you must be careful not to let them overwhelm the fruit.

BLACKBERRY CHUTNEY

Ingredients

3 pounds blackberries
1 pound cooking apples,
*   peeled and chopped*
1 pound onions, finely chopped
1/2 tablespoon salt
1 tablespoon mustard seeds
1 tablespoon ground ginger
1 tablespoon ground mace
1/4 teaspoon cayenne
1 pound brown sugar
6 cups white wine vinegar

Combine all the ingredients in a saucepan and bring to a boil. Simmer for about 1 hour or until thick. Spoon into sterilized jars, cover and label.

CAPSICUM (SWEET PEPPER) & TOMATO CHUTNEY

Ingredients

3 pounds tomatoes,
*   skinned and roughly chopped*
5 large red sweet peppers (capsicums),
*   seeded and cut into large pieces*
1 pound cooking apples,
*   peeled and chopped*
3 onions, finely chopped
1 tablespoon salt
3 cups sugar
1 1/2 quarts white vinegar
1 tablespoon allspice berries, crushed
1 tablespoon mustard seeds
5 peppercorns
2 chilies
1 tablespoon freshly grated ginger root

Put all the ingredients into a saucepan and simmer for about 2 hours or until thick. Spoon into sterilized jars, seal and label.

CELERY & TOMATO CHUTNEY

Ingredients
1 bunch celery, chopped
6 tomatoes, skinned and chopped
1 chili, chopped
1 cup sugar
1 tablespoon salt
1 teaspoon mustard seeds
1 teaspoon allspice berries, crushed
3 cloves, ground
1 cup vinegar

Combine all the ingredients in a saucepan, bring to a boil, and simmer for about an hour or until thick. Ladle into sterilized jars, seal and label.

CHAYOTE CHUTNEY

Ingredients
3 chayotes, peeled and diced
2 cooking apples, peeled and chopped
2 onions, chopped
4 cloves garlic, finely chopped
1 tablespoon grated ginger root
1 teaspoon mustard seeds
1 teaspoon fennel seeds
2 chilies, chopped
3 cloves
1/2 cup golden raisins
1 1/2 cups brown sugar
1 1/2 cups malt vinegar
1 tablespoon salt

Put all the ingredients into a large saucepan and simmer for about an hour or until the chutney thickens. Spoon it into sterilized jars, seal and label.

Try celery and tomato chutney with an appetizer of endive and ham. The tastes are complementary.

LEMON CHUTNEY

Ingredients

4 medium-sized lemons
4 medium-sized onions, chopped
1 cup golden raisins
1 cup raisins
3 chilies, finely chopped
2 cups sugar
3 cups white vinegar

Pare the zest thinly off the lemons, and chop it finely. Then squeeze the lemons for the juice. Combine all the ingredients in a bowl, and leave to stand for a few hours. Put the mixture into a saucepan, simmer until chutney is thick and sticky. Ladle into sterilized jars and seal.

LEMON & MUSTARD SEED CHUTNEY

Ingredients

5 lemons, sliced
3 onions, sliced
1 cup golden raisins
1 teaspoon allspice berries, crushed
2 bay leaves, crushed and torn
1 tablespoon mustard seeds
1 cups sugar
1 tablespoon salt
2 1/2 cups cider vinegar

Be sure to discard all the seeds from the lemon slices. Sprinkle the slices with salt and leave them in a strainer for 24 hours, then wash them.

Combine all the ingredients in a saucepan and bring to a boil. Simmer for about 40 minutes or until it thickens. Ladle into sterilized jars, seal, and store in a dark place. Try in 6 weeks.

LIME & DATE CHUTNEY

Ingredients

10 red chilies
1 tablespoon mustard seeds
2 cups vinegar
6 limes, each cut into 16 pieces
1 pound dates, pitted
1 cup raisins
10 cloves garlic, finely chopped
2 tablespoons finely chopped ginger root
1 1/2 cups sugar

Soak the chilies and mustard seeds in the vinegar for 2 hours. Combine all of the ingredients in a saucepan and bring to a boil. Slowly simmer for about 45 minutes or until it is thick and sticky. Ladle into sterilized jars, seal and store in a dry place.

MANGO CHUTNEY

Ingredients
6 large mangoes
Salt
6 cloves garlic, chopped
2 cups sugar
2 apples, peeled and chopped
12 ounces golden raisins
1 tablespoon mustard seeds
1 tablespoon finely chopped ginger root
2 cups wine vinegar
6 red chilies, finely chopped

Wipe the mangoes, before peeling and slicing them, and then removing the stones. Sprinkle them with some salt. Leave for 24 hours in a warm place. Wash, and discard excess liquid. Bruise the sliced mangoes – this helps to soften them if they are green.

Place the remaining ingredients in a saucepan. Stir over low heat until the sugar is dissolved. Add the sliced mangoes, and cook for 30 minutes or until the chutney is thick. Ladle into sterilized jars, and cover. When cool, label and store in a cool place.

Mango chutney is perfect with spicy chicken and rice.

ZUCCHINI & APPLE CHUTNEY

Ingredients

4 pounds zucchini, peeled and chopped
        into small pieces
2 pounds cooking apples,
        peeled and chopped
3 onions, finely chopped
2 cups sugar
1 1/2 tablespoons salt
1 teaspoon chopped chilies
1 tablespoon chopped ginger root
1 tablespoon black peppercorns
1 tablespoon allspice, bruised
1 1/2 quarts vinegar

Place zucchini in a bowl, sprinkling salt as you layer it. Leave for 24 hours, drain, and wash well. Put zucchini in a saucepan along with the rest of the ingredients, bring to a boil and simmer until chutney thickens. Spoon it into jars, seal, and store for at least 4 weeks before opening.

ORANGE CHUTNEY

Ingredients

5 oranges
2 cooking apples, peeled and chopped
1 cup raisins
2 tablespoons grated ginger root
3 red chilies, chopped
1 tablespoon salt
5 peppercorns, crushed
5 allspice berries, crushed
1 1/2 cups sugar
1 1/2 cups white vinegar

Pare the oranges with a potato peeler and finely chop the peel. Remove the pith and seeds, chop the flesh. Combine all the ingredients in a saucepan, bring to a boil, and simmer for about an hour or until it thickens. Spoon the chutney into hot sterilized jars, seal and label.

PEACH CHUTNEY

Ingredients
2 pounds peaches, peeled and sliced
3 onions, finely chopped
2 cups vinegar
1 cup sugar
1 tablespoon allspice berries, crushed
1 tablespoon cloves
1 tablespoon coriander seeds
3 bay leaves
5 chilies, chopped
1 tablespoon finely chopped ginger root
12 peppercorns, crushed

Combine all ingredients in a saucepan, and boil for 20 minutes or until the mixture thickens. Spoon into heated jars and seal. Keep refrigerated after opening the jar.

PEAR & WALNUT CHUTNEY

Ingredients
3 pounds pears, peeled and chopped
1 cup walnuts, chopped
2 large cooking apples,
*   peeled and chopped*
1 cup golden raisins
1 tablespoon chopped ginger root
1 teaspoon allspice berries, bruised
1 teaspoon coriander seeds
2 red chilies
1 cup sugar
1 1/2 cups wine vinegar

Combine all the ingredients in a large saucepan and bring slowly to a boil, stirring occasionally.

Simmer for about an hour or until the chutney thickens and you can draw a wooden spoon through it without any running liquid.

Ladle into sterilized jars, label, and store for at least 4 weeks before opening.

Pineapple chutney is delicious with cold meats and spicy Indian dishes. It is also delicious with freshly carved ham

PINEAPPLE CHUTNEY

Ingredients
1 cup white wine vinegar
1 cup sugar
2 teaspoons salt
1 1/2 tablespoons finely chopped ginger root
1 teaspoon ground cinnamon
2 chilies (or to taste)
2 cloves garlic, finely chopped
2 cups diced fresh pineapple
2 Granny Smith apples, peeled and cut into pieces
1/2 cup raisins

Put the vinegar, sugar, salt, ginger, cinnamon,chilies and garlic in a saucepan and bring to a boil. Add the pineapple, apples and raisins. Boil slowly, stirring often, until the apple is broken up and the chutney is thick. The pineapple will remain in pieces. Pour into warm jars and seal.

PLUM CHUTNEY

Ingredients

1 tablespoon salt
1 teaspoon ground cloves
1 teaspoon mustard seeds
1 teaspoon ground ginger
1 teaspoon ground allspice
2 red chilies
3 cups white wine vinegar
2 pounds plums, pitted
2 cups apple, peeled and sliced
2 cups onions, sliced
2/3 cups golden raisins
1 cup carrot, shredded
2 cups sugar

Put the salt, spices and vinegar in a saucepan and bring slowly to a boil. Add the remaining ingredients and stir until the mixture comes to a boil. Simmer until it thickens. Spoon into jars, seal and label. Store for 2 months before opening.

PRUNE CHUTNEY

Ingredients

2 pounds prunes
1 pound onions, finely chopped
1 tablespoon chopped ginger root
1/2 teaspoon cayenne
1 tablespoon mustard seeds
1 teaspoon coriander seeds
1 teaspoon black peppercorns
1 teaspoon allspice
3 cups malt vinegar
2 cups sugar

Soak prunes for 24 hours in just enough water to cover them. Drain, remove pits, and chop. Combine all the ingredients in a saucepan and simmer until the mixture thickens. Put at once into sterilized jars, seal, and store in a dark place.

Remember that chutneys are best if cooked so they are still a bit runny; if they are too solid they dry up too quickly.

COOK'S NOTES:
Runny liquid on the top of chutney means the chutney has not absorbed the vinegar properly and needs more cooking.

Put all the ingredients into a saucepan, bring to a boil, simmer until the mixture thickens, which should take about 50 minutes. This chutney needs to be stirred towards the end, as it gets sticky. Spoon into sterilized jars, seal and label.

RHUBARB & DATE CHUTNEY

Ingredients

4 pounds rhubarb, chopped
1 pound dates, pitted and chopped
1 pound onions, finely chopped
1 tablespoon grated ginger root
1 tablespoon allspice berries, crushed
1 tablespoon coriander seeds, crushed
6 black peppercorns, crushed
2 chilies
2 bay leaves, crushed
1 tablespoon salt
3 cups sugar
4 1/2 cups vinegar

Combine all the ingredients in a saucepan, bring to a boil, and simmer for 2 hours or until the mixture thickens. (If a spoon is drawn through, it shouldn't leave any running liquid). Ladle into sterilized jars, seal and label.

Rhubarb and dates are an excellent, tasty combination for a spicy chutney.

PUMPKIN & TOMATO CHUTNEY

Ingredients

2 1/2 pounds pumpkin, peeled and cut
into large bite–sized pieces
6 tomatoes, skinned and chopped
3 onions, chopped
1 cup raisins
2 cups sugar
1 tablespoon salt
2 tablespoons chopped ginger root
12 black peppercorns
1 tablespoon allspice berries, crushed
4 cloves garlic, crushed and chopped
1 quart white vinegar

GREEN TOMATO CHUTNEY

Ingredients

*4 pounds green tomatoes,
    peeled and chopped*
1 pound apples, peeled and chopped
4 medium onions
1 cup dates, pitted and chopped
1 cup golden raisins
2 tablespoons chopped ginger root
15 red chilies
2 cups sugar
1 tablespoon salt
3 cups vinegar

Place all the ingredients in a large
saucepan. Bring to a boil and simmer
for about 2 hours or until the chutney
thickens. Spoon into sterilized jars, seal
and label. Store in a cool, dark place.

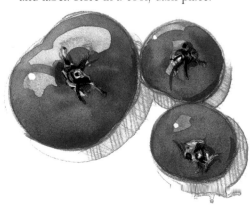

TOMATO CHUTNEY

Ingredients

*4 pounds tomatoes,
    peeled and roughly chopped*
20 cloves garlic, roughly chopped
2 tablespoons chopped ginger root
1/2 cup raisins
1 1/2 cups sugar
1 tablespoon salt
2 chilies
Zest and juice of 1 lemon
1/2 teaspoon cumin seeds
1/2 teaspoon fennel seeds
1/2 teaspoon fenugreek
1 1/2 cups white wine vinegar

Combine all the ingredients in a saucepan,
bring to a boil, and simmer for about
1 1/2 to 2 hours, stirring frequently, or until
the chutney is thick. The cooking time
depends on how firm the tomatoes are; if
they are watery, it will take longer to cook.
Spoon into sterilized jars and seal.

COOK'S NOTES:
Fruit and vegetables
are important sources
of vitamin C, among
other vital nutrients.
It is important that the
goodness is preserved
when you cook them.
Care should be taken
that the fruit and
vegetables used are
fresh and preparation
is as fast as possible.
Do not soak them in
water for a long time.

MICROWAVE CHUTNEYS

By making tomato chutney, (always a firm favorite) throughout the year, you will find the planning of Christmas gifts for friends easier.

These recipes are fast to make. Chutneys thicken at the end of cooking and need watching carefully.

DATE & APPLE CHUTNEY

Ingredients

1 1/2 pounds cooking apples,
    peeled, cored and chopped
1 pound dates, pitted and chopped
1/2 pound onions, finely chopped
1 1/2 cups brown sugar
3/4 cup golden raisins
1 teaspoon salt
1 teaspoon ground ginger
2 cloves garlic, chopped
1/2 teaspoon cayenne
2 1/2 cups white wine vinegar

Place all ingredients in a bowl, cover and cook on a high setting for 35 to 45 minutes or until thickened, stir every 10 minutes. Leave to cool slightly, then ladle into jars. Cover, seal, label and store in a dark place.

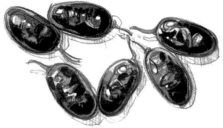

TOMATO CHUTNEY

Ingredients

1 1/2 pounds tomatoes,
skinned and quartered
1/2 pound onions, finely chopped
3/4 cup brown sugar
3/4 cup golden raisins
1 teaspoon salt
1 teaspoon ground allspice
1 teaspoon mustard seeds, ground
2 chilies, chopped
1 1/4 cups malt vinegar

Place all the ingredients in a large bowl, cover and cook on the highest setting for 35 to 45 minutes or until thickened, stirring every 10 minutes.

Leave to cool slightly, then ladle into sterilized jars. Cover, seal and label and store in a cool place.

RHUBARB CHUTNEY

Ingredients

1 pound rhubarb, chopped
1 pound dates, pitted and chopped
1 large onion, chopped
3/4 cup brown sugar
1 1/4 cups wine vinegar
2 teaspoons chopped ginger root
1 teaspoon ground ginger
1 chili, chopped

Place all the ingredients in a very large bowl and mix well. Cover and cook on the highest setting for about 30 minutes or until thickened, stirring every 10 minutes.

Leave to cool slightly, ladle into sterilized jars. Cover, seal and label in the usual way.

COOK'S NOTES:
The fruit and vegetables for chutneys and jams don't need to be the finest quality, so buy cheaply. As long as they are firm, sound and unblemished they will be perfect for preservation.

FRESH CHUTNEYS

CILANTRO CHUTNEY

Ingredients

1 cup chopped fresh cilantro
1 hot green chili
1/2 teaspoon salt
1 teaspoon roasted cumin seeds, ground
1 tablespoon lemon or lime juice
1 tablespoon grated ginger root
1 cup yogurt

Put all the ingredients except the yogurt into a food processor and blend to a smooth paste.

   Put the yogurt into a bowl and whisk smooth. Fold in the cilantro paste with the yogurt, and refrigerate until ready to serve.

Variation: This chutney can also be used as a dip for fresh vegetables as a starter to a meal. Add more yogurt if it is too thick for a dip.

COCONUT CHUTNEY

Ingredients

1 cup desiccated coconut
1 chili, finely chopped
3 scallions, finely chopped
1 tablespoon lime or lemon juice
2 tablespoons hot milk
1/2 teaspoon salt

Mix all the ingredients together and serve in a small bowl accompanied by a bowl of fresh cilantro or mint.

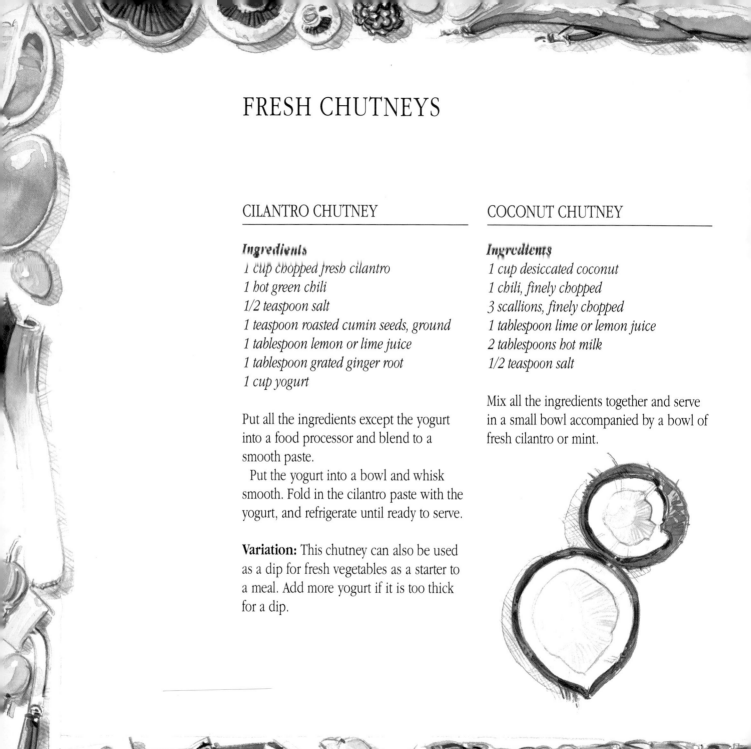

FRESH APPLE & MINT CHUTNEY

Ingredients

1 cup fresh mint leaves
2 tablespoons lemon juice
2 red chilies
1 green apple, peeled and diced
        (keep it in the lemon juice)
1 orange, peeled, seeded and cubed
1 teaspoon salt

Combine all the ingredients in a blender and blend to a smooth paste. Cover and refrigerate until serving.

Variation: Try making this with cilantro leaves instead of mint, for delicious results. Add a little coriander seed and cumin which has been roasted and freshly ground.

FRESH GREEN CHUTNEY

Ingredients

1 cup mint or cilantro leaves
1 green chili
2 tablespoons lemon juice
2 scallions, finely chopped
Pepper
1 teaspoon sugar
1/2 teaspoon salt

Blend the cilantro and chili with the lemon juice in a food processor. Combine this paste with the rest of the ingredients in a bowl. Refrigerate until ready to serve.

Besides being a traditional part of an Indian meal, this apple and mint chutney can be served as a salad accompanying any meat dish.

Walnut chutney is a very popular fresh Indian chutney. It makes an excellent appetizer, too. Just add yogurt and serve with crusty bread.

SESAME SEED CHUTNEY

Ingredients
6 tablespoons sesame seeds
2 cloves
3 scallions, chopped
1 tablespoon finely chopped
red pepper (capsicum)
2 tablespoons lemon juice
A pinch of cayenne
1/2 teaspoon salt

Toast the sesame seeds in a dry skillet until they begin to turn color. Put them in a food processor with the other ingredients. Blend to a thick paste and refrigerate in a small bowl.

WALNUT CHUTNEY

Ingredients
1 cup shelled walnuts
1 red chili, chopped
A pinch of salt
1/2 cup yogurt

Grind the walnuts, chili and salt in a food mill or food processor until smooth. Whisk the yogurt in a bowl until smooth, then mix in the walnut paste. Refrigerate until ready to serve.

YOGURT CHUTNEY

Ingredients
2 cups yogurt
2 tablespoons chopped fresh cilantro
2 tablespoons finely chopped fresh mint
2 tablespoons finely chopped onions
1/2 tablespoon chopped garlic
1 red chili, chopped
A pinch of pepper
A pinch of salt

Whisk the yogurt in a bowl until smooth. Mix all ingredients into the bowl, refrigerate. Garnish with cilantro leaves.

COOK'S NOTES:
Keep chutneys and pickles refrigerated after opening the jars. When taking fruits and chutneys from storage in the refrigerator, leave for 1 hour before eating them.

PICKLES

PICKLING VINEGAR

Ingredients
1 tablespoon mustard seeds
1 tablespoon coriander seeds
1 tablespoon allspice berries
1 teaspoon peppercorns
1 tablespoon salt
1 to 3 red chilies
2 bay leaves, crushed
A few pieces of ginger root
2 quarts white vinegar

Combine all the ingredients in a saucepan, bring to a boil, then simmer for about 10 minutes. Spoon into sterilized bottles, seal and label.

You may prefer to tie the spices up in a cheesecloth bag and remove the bag at bottling stage. To make the bottle look more attractive, add, when appropriate, garlic cloves or fennel seed stalks, small celery leaves, beet slices to turn the vinegar pink, and herbs.

There are endless combinations, and it is fun to experiment.

PICKLED BEETS

Ingredients
12 medium beets
2 tablespoons chopped celery stalks and small leaves
3 cups white vinegar
1/2 cup sugar
1 tablespoon allspice berries, crushed
3 cloves
12 black peppercorns
3 cloves garlic

Cook the beets in boiling water for about 50 minutes or until tender. The timing depends on how big they are. Peel and slice the beets before packing them into warm sterilized jars with pieces of celery and leaves in between.

In the meantime, put the vinegar, sugar and spices into the saucepan, bring to a boil, and simmer for 5 minutes only. Let the liquid stand for several hours before pouring it, strained, over the beet slices. You may omit the standing period if you are not straining off the spices.

COOK'S NOTES: If the chutney shrinks in the jar after a month, it means it has not been covered properly. Chutneys should be sealed with a plastic-lined metal lid or plastic lid. Jam covers and paper covers are not enough to prevent the vinegar evaporating. You can put paper and fabric covers over the plastic lid to make it more attractive.

BREAD & BUTTER PICKLES

Ingredients

16 cups cucumbers, sliced 1/4 inch thick
1 pound onions, thinly sliced
1/2 cup salt
Water
Ice cubes
3-4 cups sugar
1 1/4 quarts cider vinegar or white vinegar
1 1/2 teaspoons fennel seeds
1 1/2 teaspoons brown mustard seeds
1 1/2 teaspoons turmeric
2 red chilies

Bread and butter pickles are a perennial favorite and so handy to have in the kitchen cupboard. The pickled turnips have a delicate mild flavor.

In a bowl, mix together the cucumbers, onions and salt. Cover with cold water and ice cubes and leave for 3 hours. Drain, rinse well and drain again. Set aside.

About 30 minutes before the cucumber mixture is ready, combine in a saucepan the sugar, vinegar, fennel, mustard seeds and turmeric. Stir over medium heat until the sugar has dissolved. Increase the heat and bring to a boil. Reduce the heat and simmer uncovered for 30 minutes or until very syrupy, stirring often.

Meanwhile, sterilize jars and lids. Add cucumbers and onions; heat but do not boil, stirring occasionally.

Ladle the hot mixture into hot jars leaving 1/2 inch head space. Using a spatula, release any air bubbles from the side and bottom of each jar. Wipe and close the jars. Store in a cool, dark place. When a jar is opened, store it in the refrigerator.

PICKLED RED CABBAGE

Ingredients

1 red cabbage, finely shredded
1 cup salt
2-3 cups pickling vinegar

Be sure to remove the coarse outer leaves of the cabbage and the thick white stalks. Put the shredded cabbage in a large bowl, sprinkling with salt as you put it in. Cover and leave for 24 hours. Drain and rinse. Put into sterilized warm jars and cover with the cold pickling vinegar. Seal and label.

Capsicum (sweet pepper) retains its rich color through the pickling process.

PICKLED RED CABBAGE & CAULIFLOWER

Ingredients
1/2 red cabbage
1 cauliflower
3 tablespoons salt
1 quart water
1 1/2 cups white vinegar
1 teaspoon caraway seeds
1 red chili
1 bay leaf

Cut the cabbage into 1/4-inch squares. Separate the cauliflower into florets. Pack the vegetables into large sterilized jars, arranging them alternately in layers. Mix the salt, water, vinegar, caraway seeds and chili together and pour over the vegetables. Seal, label and store. It will be ready to eat in a week. Keep no longer than 2 months.

PICKLED CAPSICUMS (SWEET PEPPERS)

Ingredients
2 pounds red peppers (capsicums)
3 1/2 tablespoons salt
4 cups water
2 cups white vinegar
3 cloves garlic
1 bay leaf
1 tablespoon fennel seeds
1 cup celery stalks and leaves, chopped

Cut the sweet peppers into large pieces, after discarding seeds and cores. Pack in a sterilized jar. Mix the other ingredients and pour over the peppers. Seal, label and store. They are ready to eat in 8 to 10 days.

COOK'S NOTES:
To peel vegetables, use a potato peeler. Before skinning tomatoes, pour boiling water on them in a bowl and let them stand for 30 seconds; then cool them under cold running water.

CABBAGE & CAPSICUM PICKLE (CSALAMADE)

Ingredients
1 small white cabbage, shredded
1 cup salt
3 green peppers (capsicums), thinly sliced
3 onions, cut into thin rings
1 1/2 tablespoons black peppercorns
2 cloves
6 bay leaves
3 cloves garlic
1/2 cup sugar
1 1/2 cups vinegar
1 1/2 cups water

Put cabbage into a bowl and sprinkle with salt. Leave for an hour. Wash the cabbage, drain, add the peppers, onions, cloves, peppercorns, bay leaves, garlic and sugar. Pack the mixture into a sterilized jar then pour over the vinegar followed by the water, up to the brim. Seal and label.

PICKLED CUCUMBERS

Ingredients
4 English cucumbers
1/2 cup salt
2-3 cups white vinegar
2 tablespoons sugar
3 chilies, chopped

Cut the cucumbers lengthways into four. Scoop out the seeds with a spoon then cut the cucumbers into cubes. Put the cubes into a bowl, sprinkle with salt and cover with water and ice cubes. Then leave for 2 hours. Drain and rinse.

Put the vinegar and sugar into a saucepan and bring to a boil. Simmer until the sugar dissolves and then add the cucumbers and chilies.
Bring to a boil again, remove from heat. It is ready to eat when cool. Lasts up to 2 weeks if bottled and refrigerated.

DILL PICKLES

Ingredients
1 pound small pickling cucumbers
2 cloves garlic
2 teaspoon dill seeds
1 teaspoon peppercorns
1 teaspoon coriander seeds
2 bay leaves
1 cup white vinegar
1 tablespoon salt

Wash the cucumbers well and pack them into sterilized jars. Distribute the garlic, dill seeds, peppercorns, coriander seeds and bay leaves around the jar.

Put the vinegar and salt into a saucepan and bring to a boil. Take off the heat and pour into the jars. Seal, label and store in a dark place. They are ready to eat in a week and last about 4 to 6 weeks. Refrigerate once the jar has been opened.

Halve the eggplant lengthways, scoop out the flesh, and chop finely. Mix with 1/2 cup vinegar to prevent discoloration.

Put the lemon juice and the remaining vinegar into a blender with the mustard, coriander and fennel seeds, garlic and ginger, and blend until smooth. Add to eggplant flesh, and season to taste with chili powder, salt and pepper.

Spoon into jars and store, covered, in the refrigerator. This savory purée will keep refrigerated for several weeks.

PICKLED EGGPLANT

Ingredients
2 medium eggplant
1 cup vinegar
1/4 cup lemon juice
2 teaspoons mustard seeds
2 teaspoons coriander seeds, toasted
1 teaspoon fennel seeds
3 cloves garlic
2 teaspoons chopped ginger root
A pinch of chili powder
Salt and pepper

Pierce the eggplant all over with a fork and place them on a rack in a preheated hot oven 400°F with a dish below to catch juices. Bake for 30 minutes or until soft.

Eggplant pickle goes well with a few slices of tomato in a warm crusty roll.

GINGER PICKLE

Ingredients
1 pound ginger root
1 red chili
1 cup sugar
3 cups white vinegar

Peel the skin off the ginger and slice it
thinly. Put the chili, sugar and vinegar into
a saucepan and bring to a boil. Add the
ginger and simmer for about 45 minutes.
Spoon into sterilized jars, label, and store
in a dark place. It will be ready in 1 week.

HONEY DEW MELON PICKLE

Ingredients
4 cups honey dew melon,
*   cut into 3/4-inch cubes*
1 1/2 cups pickling vinegar
2 cups sugar
1 tablespoon grated ginger root
2 cloves garlic, finely chopped

Bring a large saucepan of water to a boil,
put in the melon, and as soon as the water
comes to a boil again, remove the fruit and
plunge it under a cold water tap to refresh.

Bring the vinegar to a boil in a saucepan,
put in the melon, and cook for 2 minutes
after the vinegar has come to a boil. Pour
the melon and vinegar into a large china
bowl, cover, and leave for 2 days. It looks
dull and cloudy at this stage. It will clear at
a second cooking.

Strain off the vinegar, bring it to a boil,
add the sugar, ginger and garlic. Now add
the melon, boil for 3 minutes, and then
take out the melon with a slotted spoon
and pack into warm jars.

Keep the syrup boiling for a while,
removing any scum that has been thrown
up. When it has cooled down slightly, pour
it over the melon.

PICKLED LIMES

Ingredients
12 limes
1/2 cup salt
5 bay leaves
1 tablespoon paprika
10 peppercorns
1 1/2 cups olive oil

Wash the limes and cut them into slices. Sprinkle them with the salt, and leave to drain in a strainer for 24 hours.

Pack the lime slices and bay leaves into sterilized jars, sprinkling the paprika and peppercorns between each layer. Cover with olive oil, seal and label. The limes should be ready to eat in 4 weeks.

MIXED PICKLES

Ingredients
2 pounds mixed vegetables: cauliflowers,
*   cucumbers, cabbages, capsicums*
*   (red or green peppers), onions,*
*   tomatoes, turnips, carrots, and*
*   green beans.*
2 cups pickling vinegar

Trim and peel the vegetables and cut into small pieces. Pack into sterilized jars, and pour hot pickling vinegar over them. Seal, label and store. They will be ready in a week. Do not keep longer than 2 months.

FRESH PICKLES

Ingredients
2 cups vinegar
1 tablespoon salt
2 pounds mixed vegetables; cauliflower,
*   cabbage, cucumbers, carrots,*
*   pickling onions, cut into*
*   small pieces*
1 onion, finely chopped
3 red chilies, finely chopped
3 cloves garlic, finely chopped
1 tablespoon finely chopped ginger root
2 tablespoons oil

Bring the vinegar and salt to a boil, and add the mixed vegetables for 1 minute. Drain. Mix the onion, chilies, garlic and ginger together. Stir fry in the oil for a few minutes, then add the vegetables and stir fry for a minute. Drain and place in a bowl. Mint leaves sprinkled on top give the dish an extra tang.

COOK'S NOTES:
An alternative method for sterilizing jars is to put them in the dishwasher without powder and use a hot cycle. This would be a bit extravagant unless you are doing a very large batch of bottling.

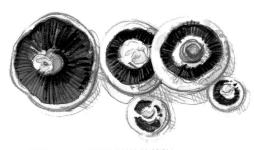

PICKLED MUSHROOMS

Ingredients
2 cups pickling vinegar
2 pounds button mushrooms
1 onion, finely chopped

Bring the pickling vinegar to a boil, add the mushrooms and onion, and simmer until tender. Spoon into warm jars and pour vinegar over. Seal, label, and store. They will be ready to eat in 2 weeks.

PICCALILLI

Ingredients
4 pounds mixed vegetables: cauliflower,
onions, green beans, cucumbers
and green tomatoes
1/2 cup salt
1 cup sugar
1 tablespoon dry mustard

1 tablespoon turmeric
3 cups vinegar
3 tablespoons cornstarch
3 chilies
1 tablespoon chopped ginger root

Cut the vegetables into small pieces. Put them into a bowl and sprinkle with salt. Leave for 24 hours, drain, and wash well.

Make a paste by mixing the sugar, mustard, turmeric and cornflour together with a little vinegar. Heat the rest of the vinegar with the chilies; when it comes to a boil, add the vegetables and simmer for 15 minutes.

Remove the vegetables and pack into sterilized jars. Add the paste to the vinegar, stirring for 5 minutes, then pour it over the vegetables.

Seal, label and store in a dark place. It will be ready to eat in a week and will last for a few months.

PICKLED PLUMS

Ingredients
3 pounds plums
1 tablespoon finely chopped ginger root
2 red chilies

COOK'S NOTES:
If there is cloudy fluid in the pickles, it means either the vegetable brine was insufficient or the spices were not strained from the vinegar.

1 teaspoon ground cloves
1 teaspoon ground cinnamon
2 tablespoons ground allspice
1 tablespoon salt
1 1/2 cups sugar
2 cups vinegar

Take the stalks off the plums, wash the fruit and prick with a needle. Put all the other ingredients into a saucepan and cook slowly until boiling, stirring occasionally. Add the plums and simmer gently for a few minutes. If the plums are too ripe, the skin will break. Spoon the plums into sterilized jars. Keep boiling the syrup until it thickens, then pour over the plums. Seal, label and store for 2 months before eating.

PICKLED ORANGES

Ingredients
4 oranges
A pinch of bicarbonate of soda
2 cups white vinegar
1 cup sugar
1 teaspoon ground cloves
1 cinnamon stick
6 cloves
4 bay leaves

Scrub the oranges and put in a saucepan with the soda and cover with water. Bring to a boil, then simmer for 20 minutes. Take the oranges out of the water and cut them into 8 wedges each.

Make a syrup with the vinegar, sugar, ground cloves and cinnamon, stirring until the sugar has dissolved. When it has come to a boil, add the orange wedges. Simmer for 15 minutes.

Place the orange wedges in sterilized jars, add the whole cloves and bay leaves, and pour the syrup over them. Seal and label. They will be ready to eat in a week.

Peel the peaches by first pouring boiling water over them; the skin should come off easily after a few minutes. To prevent discoloration, keep the peaches in water with the juice of a lemon until needed.

Put the cinnamon, nutmeg, ginger, allspice, sugar, water and vinegar into a saucepan, then bring to a boil. Simmer for 10 minutes. Stud each peach with 2 cloves, and put them into the syrup. Simmer for a few minutes until tender.. Pack into jars.

Keep boiling the syrup until it begins to thicken, then pour over the peaches. Seal, label and store. Eat after 6 weeks.

PICKLED PEARS

Ingredients
2 pounds pears, peeled,
cored and quartered
Juice of half a lemon
1 tablespoon cloves
1 teaspoon allspice berries
1 teaspoon coriander seeds
1 teaspoon finely sliced ginger root
1 cinnamon stick
1 piece lemon peel
2 cups sugar
2 cups vinegar

Make pickled pears when the fruit is cheap. The resulting mixture is deliciously fresh and tasty.

PICKLED PEACHES

Ingredients
4 pounds small peaches
1 cinnamon stick
1 nutmeg, grated
1 tablespoon finely sliced ginger root
1 teaspoon allspice berries, crushed
3 cups sugar
3 cups water
3 cups white vinegar
1 tablespoon cloves

When peeling and quartering the pears, place them in a bowl with water and the lemon juice to prevent discoloration. Stud each piece with a clove.

Place the spices, lemon peel, sugar and vinegar in a saucepan. Bring to a boil, and add the pears. Simmer until tender. Spoon pears into sterilized jars. Keep cooking the syrup until it thickens; then pour it over the pears. Seal, label and store. They will be ready to eat in 2 weeks.

SPICED QUINCES

Ingredients

6 quinces, peeled, cored and cut
*   into 8 pieces each*
1 tablespoon salt
1 1/2 cups sugar
1 cup white vinegar
2 teaspoons coriander seeds
1 teaspoon allspice berries

Cover the quince pieces with water and a tablespoon of salt. Boil for 10 minutes and strain to make 3 cups of juice.

Add the sugar, vinegar, coriander and allspice to the juice in a saucepan and bring to a boil. Put in the fruit and simmer until it is tender, then remove from the heat and leave in the saucepan for 12 hours.

Drain off the syrup, bring it to a boil, and pour over the quinces placed in sterilized jars. Seal, label, and store in a dark place.

These spiced quinces last a long time. They taste good with cold chicken or ham.

PICKLED TURNIPS

Ingredients

2 pounds small white turnips, quartered
Some celery leaves
4 cloves garlic
2 cloves
10 peppercorns
1 raw beet, sliced
3 tablespoons salt
2 cups water
2 cups vinegar

Put the turnips into sterilized jars along with the celery leaves, garlic, cloves, peppercorns and beet.

Mix the salt, water and vinegar together and pour over the turnips. Seal, label and store in a warm place.

They will be ready to eat in 10 days, but will keep no longer than 6 weeks.

HOMEMADE GIFTS

HOMEMADE GIFTS

We all love to give presents and to receive them. A prettily wrapped, mysterious package is always exciting. If it is a homemade gift, it is all the more exceptional. The thoughtfulness and the time spent on creating it go toward making the recipient feel very special.

Nearly everyone appreciates good food. It is not only one of the necessities of life but one of the great delights. When you give an edible gift you give something to be savored. Homemade gifts cost less than bought ones. A full bottle of fruit liqueur can be made with half a bottle of the cheapest brandy or gin and some fruit and sugar–not very expensive, and so delicious. Make pickles, chutneys and fruit liqueur's when there is a glut of plums, cherries or oranges in the markets. Plan to make presents all through the year, taking advantage of gluts and making use of windfalls, and you will always have edible gifts. Most chutneys, fruit preserves and liqueur's improve with age.

Some of the recipes in this collection are for edibles that should be consumed soon after they are made, such as the pear and rum sauce (to serve with Christmas plum pudding) and the country-style pâté. Others are for special occasions: a delicious fruit Christmas cake, Easter cookies and St Valentine cookies.

You will find plenty of ideas among the recipes for presents: gingerbread men and coconut macaroons for children, cherries in brandy for your best friend. There are curry pastes for making authentic indian curries; olive paste to take as a gift for a barbecue lunch for the chef; pineapple marmalade to put under the Christmas tree as a thank-you gift for the next-door neighbors; and edible gifts from a country garden, such as a bouquet of herbs, aromatic herbs for the barbecue and herbal teas.

GIFTS FROM THE COUNTRY KITCHEN

CONTAINERS
Making gifts through the year requires some planning ahead. Containers are an important consideration. Recycle all your bottles and jars, especially finely shaped ones. Train 'non-cooking' friends and

family to donate their bottles and jars. Wash bottles and jars very thoroughly and take off the old labels before storing. Stubborn labels can be removed with lighter fluid. When you bring the bottles and jars out for use, wash and rinse them again and sterilize them just before they are needed. The easiest method of sterilizing glass containers is to place them in a slow oven 225°F for 20 minutes. Use jars with plastic screw tops; metal should not be used, as it corrodes.

Keep attractive boxes, coffee cans, cake tins and any sort of attractive container that could be recycled. Paste paper over boxes and tins that are a great shape but have ugly advertising on them. Try painting them. Explore antique markets for cheap old glass bottles and jars, pieces of china, interesting old tins or boxes.

Buy good preserving jars with screw tops and bottles with metal-wired glass lids and rubber rings. They last for ever and look attractive on the kitchen shelves.

Small straw baskets are not expensive to buy and make perfect containers for many gifts, such as Easter eggs and gingerbread men. For special gifts, it is worth while buying new boxes; they come in all shapes and sizes covered with decorative paper.

*Opposite page:
Tarragon vinegar and other herb vinegars make especially good gifts. Always be on the lookout for attractive antique bottles.*

PAPER

It is not necessary to buy expensive paper. Brown paper, cellophane and tissue paper, even newspaper and white wallpaper, can look attractive as packaging. Cut out with pinking shears for an interesting edge. Paint a bright pattern in poster paints over newspaper or brown paper — or ask your children to paint it for you.

Make potato prints on newspaper and brown paper. It is easy to do. Simply cut a potato in half and draw the pattern you want on the surface. Cut away about 1/4 inch from the pattern, leaving it raised. Mix some poster paint with water in a saucer and dip the potato in. Have the paper ready, and print away. Black and gold look handsome on brown paper or red and green print up well for Christmas. If you are unsure of your skills in drawing a pattern, trace one off something you like. Print cards and labels with the same pattern.

Save all the gift wrapping paper and cards you receive and recycle them. Cut out some of the best designs and paste them down on a gift as a label or card. Save ribbons as well and press them with an iron to remove the creases. Create a ribbon basket and quite soon you will have hundreds of different shades and widths. Kitchen string looks great.

Use gift wrapping paper to cover the lids of recycled jars as well. Also save fabric for jam and chutney covers. Choose a satin ribbon to tie the cover in place. Glue the paper or fabric onto the lid so it does not come off after the bottle is opened.

Harmonize colors of the preserves with the lid and ribbon and final wrapping paper. Add a few flowers or herbs to the ribbon bow for a final country-style flourish.

LABELS

Labels are a most important element. Never forget to label a jar as soon as you seal it up. Buy pretty stickers with teddy bears or angels on them and Beatrix Potter characters for the jars of gifts for children. Attractive labels are fairly cheap to buy, but you can easily make them. Write the name of the contents, the date it was made and perhaps the recommended 'eat-by' date. It is thoughtful to present a recipe to make with presents like plum sauce or Thai red curry paste.

GIFTS FROM A COUNTRY GARDEN

A BOUQUET OF HERBS

What could be nicer to give than a fresh herbal bouquet? Arranged attractively so that all the subtlety of the individual species can be seen, it is a delight to the eye as well as the senses. You can use it now or later, fresh or dried.

The varying textures and shades of herbs look most attractive together. They need a strong design element to hold the bouquet together–a ribbon, a paper doily or cellophane paper. Try to have some herb flowers in the bouquet if possible. Study the textures and arrange leaves so that they stand out against each other but still harmonize.

Tiny herb bouquets in front of each place setting make a very attractive table decoration. Encourage your guests to take them home.

TUSSIE MUSSIE

The tussie mussie, or nosegay, is another pretty bouquet, but of herbs and cottage garden flowers, dried or fresh. Tussie mussies were carried even up to the Victorian era to disguise the dreadful smell in the towns and cities and as a protection from disease. Aromatic herbs such as rosemary, thyme and lavender were the first disinfectants. Here are a few ideas for tussie mussies:

A bouquet of herbs makes a thoughtful gift to a gourmet cook.

Rose Salad Bouquet

Start with a few roses in bud, some sage, basil, thyme, violets, some long strands of lemon peel and surround with watercress. Cut a hole in the center of a doily, poke the stem through it and tie the whole bouquet together, trimming the ends. Rose petals and violets are delicious in a salad.

Fresh Salad Bouquet

Put together basil, nasturtium flowers and leaves, romaine leaves, some mint and sorrel and surround them with spinach leaves. Tie and cut the stalks evenly. Wrap the bouquet in waxed paper and string.

Dried Tussie Mussie

This bouquet starts off fresh; but all the herbs dry very well, so they can be used for a long time to eat from as well as to perfume the room.

Gather together thyme, sage, lavender in flower, rosemary and oregano, and surround them with bay leaves. Arrange the leaves so they contrast each other. Trim the stalks. If you are giving the bouquet to a special friend, use a lace handkerchief instead of a doily to contain it and tie with a pastel satin ribbon. No need to cut a hole in the handkerchief!

Bouquet Garni

Make a pretty bunch of the classic herbs used to flavor soups and casseroles. They can be picked out of the bouquet as needed. Bay leaves, thyme, rosemary, tarragon, fennel stalks – put together a large bouquet of these herbs, dried or fresh. Surround them with lemon and orange peel and plants that do not dry successfully, such as tiny carrots, parsley, and celery tops, so they can be used fresh.

The classic bouquet garni comprises bay leaves, thyme and parsley, but other herbs can be substituted. Fennel and lemon peel taste good with fish dishes; rosemary and tarragon are added for lamb and chicken; orange peel for meat dishes.

Wrap in brown paper cut with pinking shears, and tie with thick gardening string.

POT OF HERBS

A living plant is a wonderful gift. It can bring pleasure for years as a visual and a culinary delight. Make up containers of mixed herbs and vegetables for friends as seedlings and cuttings in spring. Transfer these to the gift pots once the plants have grown.

Put seedlings in terracotta pots, the older the better. Always use a good light potting

compost, and remember to water frequently, as pots dry out quickly. Give them liquid fertilizer every 2 weeks while they are growing. Label them if necessary.

Some potting suggestions: cherry tomatoes surrounded by basil; parsley, chives and sorrel; rosemary, salad burnet and parsley; basil, bronze fennel and cilantro; spinach and cherry tomatoes; sage, oregano and tarragon; marjoram and savoury; chives and sage; a small bay tree with thyme as a ground cover; a lemon tree surrounded with basil.

Some herbs and plants are better in their own pots, as they tend to overwhelm their companions. Lemon grass and strawberries are among those best on their own.
Gift wrap the pot base with brown paper, cellophane or newspaper and tie with string or satin ribbon. You may need to put some plastic under the pot first to stop the moisture from dripping through. Add a card with a description of the plants; giving some information about how to care for them and perhaps also providing a recipe or two for their use.

AROMATIC BARBECUE MIXTURE

Fresh herbs thrown into the barbecue while the meat is cooking can enhance the flavour of the meat besides adding an extra pungency to stir the taste buds while you wait. The oils from the fresh herbs give out a powerful scent. Once the herbs are dried, they are rather like potpourri and should be thrown on the barbecue just a bit before eating, as their aroma does not last very long.

A bowl of aromatic herbs, fresh or dried, makes a lovely, thoughtful gift. Make up mixtures of any of the following herbs: rosemary, thyme, marjoram, fennel stalks, oregano, garlic, lavender, sage, savory, and bay leaves. Other aromatics that will mix with these herbs are orange and lemon peel; eucalyptus leaves and pine needles. Add some spices; juniper berries, sticks of cinnamon, star anise, whole cloves, coriander seeds and fennel seeds. Put the mixture into bowls, screw-top jars or cellophane bags tied with a bow.

An attractive spicy tea mixture which looks as attractive as it tastes. It is good to experiment with original blends of tea types.

HERBAL TEAS

Herbal teas are a pleasant change from coffee and China or Indian tea. They make a lovely present as a box of dried teas. As a rule, herbal teas are composed of individual herbs, but a mixture or the addition of spices can be very interesting. Among the herbs you can dry and use for teas are seeds from dill and fennel, lemon grass, lemon verbena, thyme, camomile, rosemary, rose hip, peppermint and sage.

Make herbal tea the same way as you make Indian tea, by infusing a spoonful in a teapot for 5 to 10 minutes.

SPICY TEA MIXTURE

Ingredients
1 1/2 cups Darjeeling tea leaves
3 star anise, crushed
2 sticks cinnamon, crushed
Peel of half a lemon, dried and chopped
3 cloves, crushed
6 peppercorns, crushed

Mix all the ingredients together and place in an airtight box or tin. On a label describe the contents. This tea is ideal to refresh the spirit.

APPETIZING GIFTS

ROSEMARY WALNUTS

Ingredients
1 1/2 tablespoons butter
1 1/2 tablespoons olive oil
3 cups shelled walnuts
4 tablespoons chopped rosemary
1/4 teaspoon cayenne
1 teaspoon salt

*Walnut paste is also
known as the 'gourmet's
peanut butter'.
It makes a delicious
sandwich spread.*

Melt the butter and oil in a saucepan and add the walnuts and rosemary. Sauté until the walnuts are golden-brown. Add the cayenne and salt and cook for 2 minutes.

Take the walnuts and rosemary out and drain on paper towels. When cool, store in a screw-top jar or cellophane bag, add fresh sprigs of rosemary. Label and wrap.

WALNUT PASTE

Ingredients
4 1/2 cups walnut pieces
2 tablespoons freshly grated
        Parmesan cheese
1 teaspoon salt
1 teaspoon ground coriander
1 teaspoon ground cumin
2 cloves garlic, crushed
2 teaspoons balsamic vinegar
2 tablespoons virgin olive oil

Heat the walnut pieces in the oven and grind them in a food processor while still warm. Add the cheese, salt, spices, garlic, vinegar and half the oil. Blend until smooth. Put into sterilized jars and pour a thin layer of oil on top to seal. Label and attach serving ideas.

Use for sandwich fingers and individual brioches, or fill celery sticks 2 inches long.

COOK'S NOTES:
Nuts and olives make delicious and filling appetizers. Added herbs or spices enhance their unique flavors.

SPICY CASHEW NUTS

Ingredients
2 cups raw cashew nuts
2 tablespoons butter
1 teaspoon salt
1 teaspoon curry powder or garam masala
1 teaspoon cumin seeds, ground
1/4 teaspoon cayenne

Melt the butter in a saucepan and sauté the cashew nuts until they are golden. Stir in the seasonings and cook for a few more minutes. Take out the cashews with a slotted spoon; drain on paper towels. When cool, store in a clean screw-top jar. Decorate the lid and label.

OLIVES

TO PRESERVE FRESH BLACK OLIVES

Choose firm olives and prick them all over with a needle. Put them on a large cane tray, sprinkle well with enough salt to coat all the olives. If you don't have a cane tray, tape a couple of layers of cheesecloth over a large tray so that there is room for the liquid to run away.

It will take up to 4 days for the olives to lose their bitterness. Shake them three times a day. You may need to add more salt towards the end. Put the olives into clean, sterilized jars and cover with olive oil. See the following recipes for interesting aromatic flavors to add:

GARLIC & THYME OLIVES

1 pound preserved olives
10 cloves garlic, cut lengthwise into strips
Thyme
Bay leaves
Olive oil

Cut an incision with a sharp knife along the length of each olive. Pack olives into jars in layers alternating with garlic and stalks of thyme. Add one bay leaf per jar. Cover with olive oil.

CHILI OLIVES

Ingredients
1 pound preserved olives
1 tablespoon red chili peppers
Olive oil

Chop the red chilies finely and scatter onto the olives as they are placed in the jars. Cover with olive oil.

BAY LEAVES & OREGANO OLIVES

Ingredients
1 pound preserved olives
4 bay leaves, broken up
1 tablespoon oregano
A piece of lemon peel
Olive oil

Combine the olives, herbs and lemon peel in jars and pour olive oil over them.

OLIVE PASTE

Ingredients
1 pound black olives
2 teaspoons finely chopped thyme
1 bay leaf, crushed and broken up
2 teaspoons salt
2 teaspoons white wine vinegar
2 teaspoons extra virgin olive oil

Pit the olives. Put all the ingredients in a food processor and blend until smooth. Store in sterilized jars. Pour a thin layer of oil on top to seal.

FAMILY GIFTS

EASTER EGGS

Ingredients
12 eggs, free range if possible
Onion skins, brown, red and white
12 pieces of cheesecloth, 6 inches square

Wrap the eggs in onion skins so that you
get all the different colors against the egg.
Wrap a piece of cheesecloth around each
egg to hold the onion skins in place.
Secure with string.

  Put the eggs in a saucepan and cover
with water. Slowly bring to a boil and
simmer for 12 minutes. Remove from heat
and let the eggs sit in the water until they
are cool. Unwrap and refrigerate.

COOKING KIT FOR KIDS

The art of fine cooking is a wonderful
possession, something that can give you
joy every day of your life. It is never too
early to teach children to cook. The
chemistry will fascinate them — the
knowledge that they actually created
biscuits from flour, butter and water. And
of course, they learn early that one's own
cooking always tastes best.

  Put together a first cook's kit for a curious
child. Into a large mixing bowl put an
apron, pastry cutters, plastic measuring
spoons and jugs, one large and one small
knife, a wooden spoon, spatula and a
rolling pin.

  Include a list of kitchen safety rules and
a few simple recipes. Some easy recipes
to start with are fruit and nut fudge (page
116), coconut chocolate (page 118),
coconut macaroons (page 120), and ginger
nuts (page 122).

SPICY FOODS

THAI RED CURRY PASTE

Ingredients
1 teaspoon peppercorns
2 teaspoons coriander seeds, roasted
2 teaspoons cumin seeds, roasted
1 teaspoon grated nutmeg
1 teaspoon ground mace
1 tablespoon chopped dried red chilies
2 tablespoons shrimp paste (kapee)
1/2 cup onions chopped
1/2 cup garlic chopped
1/2 cup chopped lemon grass or lemon peel
1 tablespoon chopped cilantro
Zest of 1 lime or lemon
1 tablespoon salt

Grind together the peppercorns, coriander and cumin seeds, nutmeg, mace and chilies. Put this powder into a food processor with the remaining ingredients and blend to a smooth paste. When packing the paste into the jars, check carefully that there are no air bubbles. Dispel any bubbles with a spatula.

Thai red curry paste is a much appreciated present, as it takes the hard work out of Thai cooking.

FOUR SPICES (QUATRE ÉPICES)

Ingredients
2 1/2 tablespoons peppercorns
1 tablespoon whole cloves
1 tablespoon freshly grated nutmeg
1 tablespoon ground ginger

Blend the peppercorns and cloves in a food mill or clean coffee grinder. Mix with the nutmeg and ginger and store.

Madras curry paste is a rich, spicy blend perfect for serving with grilled masala chicken.

Take the skin and fat off the chicken pieces. Combine all the other ingredients in a bowl and mix well. Coat the chicken pieces with the marinade and let them marinate for at least an hour or preferably overnight in the refrigerator.

Preheat the broiler. Broil the chicken pieces for 10 to 15 minutes on one side. Turn over and cook for a further 10 to 15 minutes. Serve straight away. Serves 4-6.

MADRAS CURRY PASTE (MADRASI MASALA)

Ingredients
1 cup coriander seeds, ground
1 tablespoon cumin seeds, ground
1 tablespoon black peppercorns, ground
1 tablespoon mustard seeds, ground
1 tablespoon turmeric
1 tablespoon salt
1 teaspoon ground cloves
2 teaspoons crushed and chopped garlic
2 teaspoons finely grated ginger root
1 1/2 teaspoons white wine vinegar
1/2 cup vegetable oil

Combine all the ingredients except the oil in a bowl and mix into a smooth paste.

MASALA CHICKEN

Ingredients
1 chicken, cut into 10 pieces
1 1/2 tablespoons madras curry paste
        (see next recipe)
1 cup yogurt
4 red chilies, chopped
1 teaspoon salt
Juice of half a lemon

Heat the oil in a pan and put the paste in. Stirring constantly, cook until the spices are cooked and the oil separates. Bottle in sterilized jars.

THAI COUNTRY-STYLE BEEF

Ingredients

2 pounds stewing steak
2 cups coconut milk
3 tablespoons Thai red curry paste
        (page 101)
2 cups water
2 sticks lemon grass, 2 3/4 inches long
1 teaspoon salt
3 red chilies, chopped

Take all the fat off the beef and cut into bite-size pieces. Put the coconut milk in a saucepan and bring to a boil. Add the curry paste; stir well for 5 minutes.

Add the meat, coating all the pieces with the sauce. Stir for 5 minutes, then add all the other ingredients. Bring to a boil, cover, and simmer slowly for 1 1/2 hours or until the beef is tender.

Add more hot water if the sauce begins to dry out. Serves 6.

COUNTRY-STYLE PATE

Ingredients

6 slices bacon
1 pound chicken livers
1 pound lean ground pork
1 egg, beaten
2 cups soft breadcrumbs
2 tablespoons brandy
2 cloves garlic, crushed
1 teaspoon chopped thyme
8 juniper berries, crushed
2 teaspoons black pepper
1 teaspoon salt
1/2 teaspoon four spices

Cut the rind from the bacon slices and line a terrine dish with them, letting the ends overhang on one side–they will be used to cover the top of the pâté. Clean the chicken livers and grind them. In a bowl, combine the ground liver with all the other ingredients and mix well. Put the mixture into the terrine dish and fold the bacon ends over the top. Cover with the lid of the terrine or foil. Put the terrine into a baking dish and add hot water to a depth of 3/4 inch to the dish.

Place in a preheated oven at 350°F for 1 1/2 hours. Cool and refrigerate.

SAUCES

RHUBARB & GINGER SAUCE

Ingredients
1 cup white wine vinegar
1 cup sugar
Zest and juice of 2 oranges
1 red chili
1 teaspoon allspice berries
1 teaspoon mustard seeds
1/2 teaspoon cinnamon
6 stalks rhubarb, washed, trimmed
*   and cut into 2 inch pieces*
Zest of 1 lemon
1 tablespoon chopped ginger root
1/2 cup golden raisins
1 teaspoon salt

Place vinegar, sugar, orange juice, chili, allspice, mustard seeds, cinnamon in a saucepan and bring to a boil.

Add rhubarb, with the zest, ginger, golden raisins and salt. Simmer for about 45 minutes or until it thickens slightly. Ladle into warm sterilized jars.

TOMATO SAUCE

Ingredients

2 pounds tomatoes, peeled
2 tablespoons olive oil
1/2 cup onion finely chopped
4 cloves garlic, finely chopped
2 tablespoons finely chopped parsley
2 tablespoons finely chopped basil
Salt and pepper

Roughly chop the tomatoes. Heat the oil in a large saucepan and add chopped onion. Stir until it is translucent.

Add garlic and cook for 1 minute. Add parsley and basil; season to taste. After it has come to a boil, simmer for an hour, stirring occasionally.

Remove from the heat and leave to stand for 30 minutes.

Put a couple of basil leaves in each sterilized jar, then pour in the sauce. Top with a thin layer of oil to seal the sauce. Label and store in a dark, cool place.

CUMBERLAND SAUCE

Ingredients

2 shallots, finely chopped
4 oranges
2 lemons
2 cups redcurrant jelly
1 tablespoon Dijon mustard
3 tablespoons red wine
2/3 cup Port
Salt and pepper

Put the shallots in a pan, cover with cold water and bring to a boil. Simmer for a few minutes and strain. Peel oranges and lemons very thinly with a potato peeler; cut the peel into julienne strips. Blanch them in the same way as the shallots. Melt redcurrant jelly in a heavy pan.

Stir in the mustard, wine, port, shallots and peel. Season with the salt and pepper, simmer for about 20 minutes, until the sauce is fairly thick. It will thicken more as it cools. Bottle and keep in a cool, dark place.

COOK'S NOTES: Homemade sauces, sweet and savory, make cooking so much faster once the sauces are made, and all you have to do is choose which one will go with the lamb, chicken or dessert of the day.

PEAR & RUM SAUCE

Ingredients
1 cup dark rum
2 tablespoons brown sugar
6 pears, cored, peeled and chopped
1 cup unsalted butter

Put half rum and sugar in a saucepan and
dissolve sugar. Add pears and stew until
soft. Blend in a food processor. Melt butter,
add purée and remaining rum. Heat until
blended. Store in a jar. Heat before serving.

PLUM SAUCE

*Make plum sauce with
windfall plums towards
the end of the season.*

Ingredients
4 pounds plums, pitted
1 cup onions finely chopped

1 1/4 quarts white wine vinegar
1 tablespoon salt
1 cup golden raisins
1/4 teaspoon cayenne
1 teaspoon crushed allspice berries
1 tablespoon grated ginger root
3 cloves garlic, crushed
1 1/2 cups granulated sugar

Put all ingredients into a large saucepan.
Bring to a boil, then gently simmer for
1 1/2 hours.
   Ladle into jars. The sauce will thicken as
it cools. Seal and label.

MUSTARD

Mustard is generally made from the seeds of black mustard (*Brassica nigra*) and white mustard (*Brassica alba*). If you haven't a food mill, use a coffee grinder to grind the seeds. Put mustard into small sterilized jars or pots and keep for 2 weeks before using. Small white porcelain bowls make a present into a gift.

BAVARIAN MUSTARD

Ingredients
2 tablespoons black mustard seeds
2 tablespoons white mustard seeds
2 tablespoons grated horseradish,
          fresh if possible
1 teaspoon salt
1 teaspoon olive oil
3 tablespoons white wine vinegar
1 teaspoon honey

Grind the mustard seeds, then put ground seeds into the blender with the other ingredients. Blend to a smooth paste. Bottle and label.

COUNTRY-STYLE MUSTARD

Ingredients
1 tablespoon black mustard seeds
3 tablespoons white mustard seeds
1 tablespoon finely chopped tarragon
1 tablespoon finely chopped parsley
1 teaspoon salt
1 tablespoon olive oil
3 tablespoons cider vinegar
1 tablespoon honey

Grind mustard seeds in a grinder and put into a blender with the rest of the ingredients. Blend to a smooth paste. Spoon into sterilized jars.

TARRAGON VINEGAR

Herb vinegars make a very attractive gift in a nicely shaped bottle. Olive oil bottles are usually a lovely shape to recycle.

Ingredients
1 cup tarragon
1 quart wine vinegar

Put the tarragon in a wide-necked jar and pour vinegar over it. Cover and leave for

COOK'S NOTES:
Save all your bottles for storing jams, chutneys and pickles. Recycle pretty material for cloth covers and ribbons. Re-use attractive wrapping paper to cover commercial boxes and coffee cans.

2 weeks, shaking the jar every day. Strain the vinegar into sterilized bottles. Add a sprig of tarragon to each bottle.

Variation: Use the same method for making marjoram, thyme, basil or rosemary vinegars.

MINT VINEGAR

Ingredients
2 cups mint leaves
1/2 cup granulated sugar
1 3/4 pints cider vinegar

Combine mint with the sugar in a sterilized bottle. Bring the vinegar to a boil and pour over the sugar and mint. Allow to stand for 10 days, shaking the bottle daily. Strain and bottle again.

SPICY OIL

Do not use the most expensive extra virgin oil for this hearty oil. A cheaper cold-pressed oil will do very well. Spicy oil is excellent to have by a barbecue for basting meats or vegetables.

Ingredients
3 red chilies
2 cloves garlic
1 teaspoon cumin seeds, ground
1 teaspoon coriander seeds, ground
5 cardamom pods
10 black peppercorns
3 cups olive oil

Put the spices into a sterilized oil bottle and pour the oil over them. Seal and label.

Cold pressed olive oil is the perfect gift for a gourmet cook.

PRESERVES TO GIVE

SPICED CHERRIES

Ingredients

2 pounds cherries, washed
2 cloves
1 teaspoon coriander seeds
1 tablespoon grated ginger root
1 cinnamon stick
1 cup granulated sugar
1 1/2 cups wine vinegar

Prick the cherries with a needle. Tie spices
in a cheesecloth bag. Put sugar, vinegar
and spices into a saucepan and bring to a
boil to dissolve sugar. Add cherries and
cook until tender. Spoon into jars and seal.

PICKLED MUSHROOMS

Ingredients

1 pound button mushrooms
Salted water
2 1/2 cups white wine vinegar
10-12 peppercorns, cracked
2 or 3 bay leaves, broken

*Pickled mushrooms are
handy to have in the
store cupboard to
enhance a buffet table
or take to a picnic.*

1 large onion, sliced
2 cloves garlic, bruised
1 sprig thyme or rosemary

Trim stems of mushroom, place in a
saucepan with salted water to cover and
bring to a boil. Remove from heat, stand
for 5 minutes, drain and dry the
mushrooms on paper towels. Combine
the vinegar with peppercorns, bay leaves,
onion, garlic and thyme in enamel
saucepan. Bring to a boil, then simmer for
5 minutes. Strain, keep spiced vinegar hot.
   Fill heated jars with mushrooms,pour in
spiced vinegar to the rim. Seal with acid-
proof seals, and store for 2 to 3 weeks.

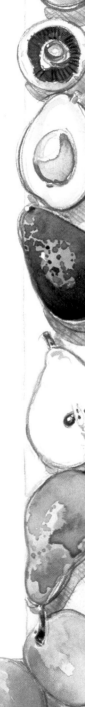

APPLE & PEAR CHUTNEY

Ingredients

1 1/2 cups granulated sugar
1 cup white wine vinegar
2 teaspoons allspice berries
1 tablespoon chopped ginger root
6 cloves garlic, crushed
1 tablespoon salt
2 red chilies
3 cups apples, peeled and chopped
3 cups pears, peeled and chopped
2 tablespoons golden raisins

Put sugar, vinegar and spices into a saucepan and bring to a boil, stirring to dissolve the sugar. Add fruits and simmer for 45 minutes; stir from time to time, in case the mixture catches on the bottom of the saucepan. When it is soft and thickened, it is ready. Ladle into sterilized jars. Seal and store in dark, cool place. Do not forget to label and date the chutney.

SPICED PRUNES

Ingredients

1 cup wine vinegar
1 cup granulated sugar
1/2 teaspoon grated nutmeg
1/2 teaspoon ground pepper
1 red chili
1 pound prunes, pitted
2 tablespoons brandy

Put the vinegar, sugar and spices in a saucepan and slowly bring to a boil, stirring to dissolve the sugar. Pack the prunes into sterilized jars and pour the syrup over them, making sure to dispel any air bubbles. Pour some brandy into the jars and seal. It is best to let the prunes mature for a few months before opening.

DATE & BANANA CHUTNEY

Ingredients
1 cup tamarind liquid
1/2 cup brown sugar
1/2 cup wine vinegar
3 red chilies, chopped
1 teaspoon cumin seeds, ground
1 teaspoon cardamom seeds, ground
1 teaspoon salt
1 cup dates, pitted and chopped
3 green bananas, sliced

Put tamarind liquid, sugar, vinegar and spices into a saucepan and bring to a boil, stirring occasionally. Add dates and bananas and bring to a boil. Simmer for about 45 minutes or until liquid is absorbed and mixture is thick. Stir to prevent chutney sticking to the saucepan. Pour into sterilized jars and seal.

PINEAPPLE MARMALADE

Ingredients
3 1/2 cups pineapple, finely chopped
3 lemons, thinly sliced
1 3/4 quarts water
4 pounds granulated sugar

Put the pineapple, lemons and water in a large saucepan and simmer for 1 1/2 to 2 hours or until the fruit is very soft.

Add the sugar and stir until it dissolves. Turn the heat up and boil very fast for about 20 minutes or until the setting point is reached. (Test the marmalade to see if it gels on a cold plate.)

Remove from the heat and leave to rest for 15 minutes, spoon into sterilized jars and seal.

COOK'S NOTES:
Never forget to label and date the jars as soon as you have filled them. Clean the outside of the jars and inside the neck before sealing, and make sure there are no air pockets. Dispel with a spatula to remove risk of bacteria developing.

GLACE CUMQUATS

Ingredients

1 pound cumquats
1 tablespoon salt
1 pound granulated sugar
2 1/2 cups water
1/2 cup granulated sugar

Day 1: Wash the cumquats well and prick each about eight times with a needle. Put them into a bowl with the salt and enough water to cover. Soak overnight.

Day 2: Put the cumquats into a saucepan with fresh water to cover and bring to a boil. Simmer until they are tender–30 to 50 minutes. Drain and put into the bowl. At the same time, make a syrup with 1 pound sugar and water. When it becomes clear, it is ready. Pour syrup over cumquats and leave to stand overnight.

Day 3: Drain the syrup off the cumquats and put it into a saucepan, adding 1/4 cup sugar. Bring to a boil and, when clear, pour over the cumquats. Leave for 48 hours.

Day 5: Repeat day 3 process.

Day 7: Drain the cumquats, reserving syrup, roll in granulated sugar and place on a wire rack and dry in a slow oven. Store in airtight tin or wide-necked bottle.

ORANGE & CHILI MARMALADE

Ingredients
2 pounds oranges, thinly sliced
Juice and zest of 1 lemon
6 cups water
6 red chilies, whole
4 pounds granulated sugar

Put the oranges, lemon and water into a large saucepan and bring to a boil. Simmer for about 1 1/2 hours or until the oranges are almost tender, add the chilies after 45 minutes.

Add the sugar and stir until it is dissolved. As soon as the marmalade comes to a boil, turn up the heat and cook very fast for about 20 minutes or until the setting point is reached. (Test for the setting point by putting a drop of marmalade onto a very cold plate. If it crinkles when pushed and doesn't run, it is ready).

Take the marmalade from the heat. Leave it to stand for 15 minutes to distribute the fruit and then ladle into sterilized jars and seal.

APPLE & ROSEMARY JELLY

Ingredients
2 pounds apples, peeled and chopped
3 tablespoons rosemary
Granulated sugar to measure
Sprigs of rosemary

Put apples and rosemary into a saucepan with just enough water to cover them. Simmer for an hour.

Strain the mixture through a jelly bag or a strainer lined with four layers of cheesecloth sitting over a large bowl. It will take 1 or 2 hours to strain. Do not touch the fruit or jelly bag, as this will cloud the jelly.

Measure the juice in a measuring jug as you ladle it into the saucepan. Add equal measures of sugar to the juice. Dissolve sugar in the juice and bring to a rapid boil. Boil until the setting point is reached. Test by dropping a small amount on a cold plate. If it gels, it is ready.

Remove from heat, skim, and immediately pour into sterilized jars. Add a sprig of rosemary to each jar. Seal and label. Do not move the jars until the jelly is firmly set.

COOK'S NOTES:
Preserve fruit and vegetables when there is a glut in the market and the prices have fallen. Take advantage of windfalls too and watch out for people who don't harvest their fruit–they are often eager to have you pick the fruit for them to save the mess of fallen fruit.

SWEETS & SWEETMEATS

CANDIED PEEL

Ingredients
Peel of 3 oranges, 3 lemons
*   and 1 grapefruit*
3 cups granulated sugar
3 cups water
1 teaspoon baking soda

Day 1: Wash the peel to remove the wax, and remove any pulp. Cut into quarters, or eighths or more if it is large fruit. Be conscious of cutting a neat shape. Dissolve the baking soda in boiling water and soak the peel for 20 minutes. Drain and rinse the peel in cold water. Cook in fresh water until the peel is tender. Drain. Put 2 cups sugar and 3 cups water in the saucepan. Stir until the sugar dissolves and it is clear. Remove from heat and put in the peel. Leave for 2 days.

Day 3: Remove the peel and add a cup of sugar to the syrup. Dissolve the sugar and bring to a boil. Drop in the peel and simmer until the peel is almost transparent. Drain the peel on racks sitting in baking sheets. Reserve the syrup. Put the peel into a very slow oven to dry. On a very hot day, the peel could be dried outside, but beware of insects.

Day 5: Bring the syrup to a boil again and dip the peel into it. Drain again and dry. Store in airtight jars.

GLACE DATES

Ingredients

3 tablespoons slivered almonds
1 tablespoon orange juice
Confectioners' sugar as needed
1 1/2 cups dates, pitted
1 1/2 cups granulated sugar
1 cup water
1 teaspoon lemon juice

Make a stuffing of the almonds, orange juice and confectioners' sugar. Keep adding the confectioners' sugar until the mixture is firm. Stuff into the dates.

Make a syrup by putting the granulated sugar, water and lemon juice in a saucepan and cooking until you can put a spoon into the syrup and then into a glass of cold water and the surface of the spoon becomes like a layer of glass; it is then

ready. Using a fine skewer, dip each date into the syrup and place on a greased baking sheet.

When the dates are all completely dry, put them into small paper cases. Layer in an airtight tin.

CANDIED SWEET POTATOES

Ingredients

2 pounds sweet potatoes
3 tablespoons butter
Juice of half a lemon
4 tablespoons brandy
2 tablespoons brown sugar

Boil sweet potatoes until they are just cooked. Peel and slice them. Place the slices on greased baking sheets.

Melt the butter, remove from the heat and add lemon juice and brandy. Brush each slice and sprinkle the sugar over.

Cook in a preheated oven at 375°F basting every 15 minutes. They take about 45 minutes to cook.

COOK'S NOTES:
Homemade sweets are very cheap to make and generally much healthier if eaten in moderation. Remember to be patient and allow yourself plenty of time for all the molding and dipping required for presenting them attractively.

FRUIT & NUT FUDGE

Ingredients
1 cup raisins
1 cup dates, pitted
1 cup dried figs
1/2 cup dried apricots
1 cup cashew nuts
3 tablespoons orange juice

Chop fruits and nuts as finely. Combine in a bowl with orange juice. Make them into balls and place each one in a paper case. Store in an airtight tin in layers with waxed paper between each layer.

Variation: Use less orange juice and a dash of brandy or rum.

CHOCOLATE & FRUIT FUDGE

Ingredients
1 tablespoon chopped dried pears
1 tablespoon chopped candied peel
2 tablespoons raisins
1 cup walnut pieces
2 tablespoons slivered almonds
1 cup dark chocolate, melted
1 tablespoon confectioners' sugar
2 tablespoons brandy

Chop the fruit and nuts in a food processor. Put them into a bowl with the chocolate and confectioners' sugar and mix the paste.

Add brandy until it becomes soft and pliable. Mold the fudge into balls and then roll them in confectioners' sugar.

Put the balls of fudge into small paper cases and keep them in an airtight tin.

APRICOT SWEETMEATS

Ingredients
1 cup dried apricots
2 tablespoons confectioners' sugar
Whole almonds

Roughly chop up the apricots in a food processor. Mix the apricot paste with the confectioners' sugar and a little water until you get a firm mixture. Roll into small balls and sprinkle with confectioners' sugar. Place an almond on each one.

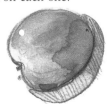

TOFFEES

Ingredients
2 pounds granulated sugar
1 cup water
1 tablespoon vinegar
1/4 teaspoon tartrate baking powder

Put all the ingredients in a large saucepan over a low heat. Stir until the sugar is dissolved. Cover with the lid for 2 minutes to prevent any sugar crystallizing on the side of the saucepan.

Remove the lid and boil rapidly until the syrup reaches 300°F. It takes about 15 minutes. The syrup turns a golden caramel color. Test by dipping half a teaspoonful into cold water for a moment or two; if it makes brittle shreds, it is ready. Be extremely careful so as to avoid burns from the hot toffee syrup. Ladle into paper cases, three-quarters filled. Sprinkle with coconut, or place an almond on the top of each toffee.

Variations:
TOFFEE BRAZIL NUTS: When making toffees, save some syrup to coat some brazil nuts. Have a cup of brazil nuts ready and a greased baking sheet. Impale the nut

COOK'S NOTES:
Keep a permanent supply of vanilla sugar by putting 2 vanilla beans in a large jar and fill it up with sugar. Top up the sugar as you use it.

on a needle and carefully dip it into hot toffee. Hold nut above syrup until it stops dripping, then push it off the needle onto the baking sheet. Store in screw-top jars.

PINE NUT BRITTLE: Follow the recipe for toffee and add 3 cups of pine nuts after the toffee reaches its correct temperature. Pour the mixture onto greased baking sheets. Let it stand until it is hard. Break into pieces and store in a sterilized jar.

TOFFEE APPLES: Put a wooden skewer into each red apple and dip into the toffee syrup. Place on greased baking sheet. Makes 20 apples.

DATE & WALNUT NOUGAT

Ingredients
1 1/2 cups dates, pitted
1 cup walnuts
3/4 cup pistachio nuts
1/2 cup superfine sugar
1/4 cup water
Juice of half a lemon
Walnut oil
Confectioners' sugar
Rice paper

Chop the dates and nuts finely in a food processor. Put the sugar and water in a saucepan and bring to a boil. When it first reaches golden brown, before the setting stage, remove from heat. Add the lemon juice, dates and nuts.

Put back on a low heat and cook for 10 minutes, stirring, then remove from the heat. When it is cool enough to handle, oil your hands and roll the mixture into logs. Leave them to harden, then roll them in confectioners' sugar. Store in layers between sheets of rice paper.

COCONUT CHOCOLATE

Ingredients
1 pound dark chocolate
1 cup desiccated coconut
1/4 teaspoon cinnamon

Melt the chocolate in a bowl by placing it in a saucepan of boiling water. Add the coconut and cinnamon and stir well. Pour into small paper cases. Sprinkle a little coconut on top. Store in layers in a tin.

HAZELNUT CHOCOLATE

Ingredients
1 pound milk chocolate
1 cup hazelnuts

Melt chocolate in a bowl placed in boiling water. Grind half the hazelnuts in a food processor and mix into chocolate. Add whole hazelnuts and stir well. When chocolate is cool enough to handle, shape into logs, then put into individual paper cases. Store in an airtight container.

other half and pour into a separate pan. It sets quickly, so keep an eye on it for the next two steps. When it is partly set, mark it into fingers. Cut when cool.

COCONUT ICE

Ingredients
2 pounds granulated sugar
1/2 cup milk
1 tablespoon butter
1 1/2 cups desiccated coconut
Pink food coloring

Combine sugar, milk and butter in a heavy saucepan and bring slowly to a boil. Stir occasionally. Boil for 5 minutes, stirring all the time. Remove from heat; add coconut. Mix well and pour half into a greased pan 1 inch deep. Put pink coloring into the

MARSHMALLOWS

Ingredients
1 1/2 cups vanilla superfine sugar
1/2 cup cold water
4 teaspoons gelatin
1/2 cup hot water
1/2 cup desiccated coconut toasted

Put sugar and cold water into a bowl and beat with an electric mixer for 4 minutes. Dissolve gelatin in hot water. Add gelatin to sugar water and beat until thick. Pour into a large pan. When cool and firm, cut into squares. Coat with desiccated coconut. Store in an airtight jar or tin.

COOKIES

EASTER COOKIES

Ingredients
1 cup flour
1/2 teaspoon salt
1 teaspoon ground cinnamon
1 teaspoon ground ginger
1/4 cup butter
4 tablespoons superfine sugar
3 tablespoons currants
1 tablespoon chopped dried apricots
2 tablespoons milk
1 egg, beaten

Sift the flour, salt and spices. Rub in the butter until the mixture resembles bread crumbs. Mix in the sugar, currants and apricots. Make a well and pour in a little milk and the beaten egg. Keep mixing and adding milk until you have a stiff dough. Refrigerate for 2 hours. Roll out the dough very thinly and cut into rounds. Put them on greased baking sheets in an oven preheated to 400°F. They will take about 20 minutes to bake. They are ready when they begin to change color.

COCONUT MACAROONS

Ingredients
2 egg whites
2 teaspoons cornstarch
4 tablespoons superfine sugar
5 tablespoons desiccated coconut
20 almonds

Beat the egg whites until they are frothy. Mix in the cornstarch and superfine sugar and then the coconut.

With a teaspoon, measure out spoonfuls of the mixture and place them on a greased baking sheet.

Put an almond on top of each, pressing down gently so that the top is slightly flattened. Bake in a preheated oven at 350°F for about 20 minutes.

They should be firm and turn a golden color. Store in an airtight tin.

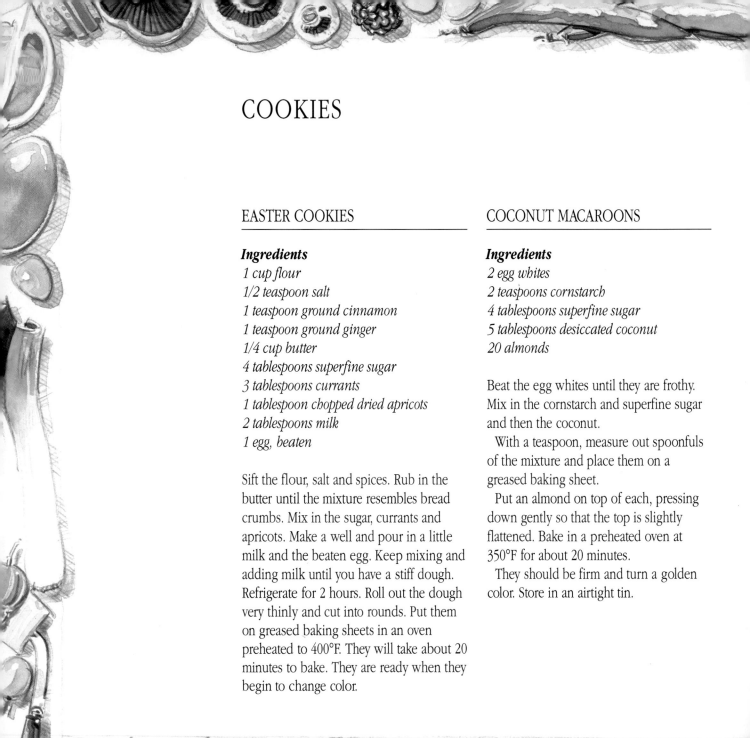

VALENTINE COOKIES

Ingredients

2 cups flour
1/2 teaspoon baking powder
3 tablespoons butter
1 cup vanilla sugar
1 egg
2 tablespoons rum
Icing
1 egg white
1 cup confectioners' sugar
1/2 teaspoon lemon juice
Red food coloring

Shortbread is a favorite with most people of all ages. Try pinching the cookie's edges for a special effect.

Sift the flour and baking powder. Cream the butter, then add the sugar gradually until light and fluffy. Add the egg and rum. Beat in flour and baking powder, a little at a time. Refrigerate dough for 2 hours.

Roll out the dough to 1/8 inch thick. Cut out the cookies with a heart-shaped cutter. Place on greased baking sheets and put in an oven preheated to 400°F. They will be ready in 10 minutes. Cool on wire racks.

To make the icing, beat egg white and add sugar gradually. Add lemon juice and red coloring. When the cookies are cool, ice with a palette knife or put the icing in a piping bag.

SHORTBREAD

Ingredients

3/4 cup butter
1/4 cup superfine sugar
2 cups flour

Cream butter and evenly add the sugar until the mixture is light and fluffy. Add flour gradually. Knead the dough for 15 minutes until smooth. Roll out dough into an 8 inch round. Make sure dough surface is smooth and even. Crimp edges of the dough and prick the surface with a fork. Bake in a preheated oven at 300°F for 20 minutes. Reduce temperature to 275°F and bake for 40 minutes. Cool on a wire rack.

GINGER NUTS

Ingredients
2 cups flour
2 teaspoon bicarbonate of soda
4 tablespoons brown sugar
1/4 cup butter
4 tablespoons light corn syrup
1 egg
2 teaspoons ground ginger
2 teaspoons ground cinnamon
15-20 almonds

Sift the flour and soda into a bowl; mix in the brown sugar. Melt the butter and light corn syrup and mix in with the dough.

Add the egg and the spices. Roll out the dough and cut into rounds. Place an almond in the middle of each one. Put on greased baking sheets in a preheated oven at 400°F. They should be ready in 15 to 20 minutes. Cool on a wire rack.

GINGERBREAD MEN

Ingredients
1/4 cup butter
1/3 cup brown sugar
1/3 cup light corn syrup
3 cups flour
1 teaspoon ground ginger
1 teaspoon cinnamon
3 teaspoons baking soda
1 egg
2 teaspoons vanilla extract

Melt the butter, sugar and syrup over a very low heat, stirring occasionally. Then allow to cool.

Sift the flour and spices into a bowl. Add the baking soda to the butter mixture. Make a well in the flour and add the butter mixture. Mix well and then add the egg and vanilla extract to make a soft dough. Roll out the dough to 1/8 inch thick. Cut out the gingerbread men with a cutter or a sharp knife.

Add currants for the eyes and a slice of candied cherry for the mouth. Put them on a greased baking sheet in a preheated oven at 325°F for 10 minutes. Cool on a wire rack.

CAKES

PANETTONE

Ingredients

1/2 cup butter
1/2 cup sugar
2 egg yolks
2 3/4 cups flour
1 teaspoon tartrate baking powder
1 teaspoon baking soda
1 egg
1 cup milk, warmed
3/4 cup golden raisins
1/2 cup candied lemon peel
Peel of 1 lemon, grated

Cream the butter until it is fluffy. Add the sugar gradually and beat until it is creamy. Beat in an egg yolk. Sift the flour, baking powder and soda. Stir in some of the flour. Beat in the second yolk, then a little flour and then the whole egg. Beat in the warm milk. Beat in the remaining flour. Mix well for about 15 minutes. Stir the golden raisins, candied peel and grated rind into the batter. Pour into a greased and floured cake pan and bake in a preheated oven at 350°F for 45 minutes. Let it cool in the tin for 10 minutes, then turn out on a wire rack. Sprinkle with confectioners' sugar.

CHRISTMAS FRUIT & NUT CAKE

Ingredients

1 cup brazil nuts
1 cup walnuts
1 cup dates, pitted
1/2 cup prunes chopped
1/3 cup chopped candied peel
1/3 cup candied cherries
1/2 cup golden raisins
Peel of 1 lemon, grated
1/2 cup brandy
3 tablespoons flour
1/2 teaspoon baking powder
1/2 cup brown sugar
3 eggs
1 teaspoon vanilla extract

Put the nuts, fruit and lemon peel into a bowl and pour in the brandy. Mix well, cover and leave to macerate for a week.

COOK'S NOTES:
Double grease a cake pan or pudding basin to be sure of success in turning out the cake or pudding. Brush melted butter over the surface. Put in the refrigerator for 10 minutes, then grease again and refrigerate. Sprinkle in a little flour just before pouring the mixture in.

Sift the flour and baking powder together and mix with the fruit and nuts. Then add the sugar, eggs and vanilla and mix well. Put into a well-greased and floured oblong pan. Smooth the top, making sure there are some nuts on the top for decoration. Cover with foil.

Put into an oven preheated to 300°F and bake for 1 1/2 to 2 hours. Take the foil off for the last 30 minutes. Leave to cool for 10 minutes in the pan, then turn out on a wire rack. Store the cake in a tin with several layers of foil around the cake. Keep in a cool place. Once opened, refrigerate.

ORANGE & ALMOND CAKE

Ingredients
2 oranges
6 eggs
1 cup ground almonds
1 cup superfine sugar
Zest of 1 lemon
1 teaspoon baking powder
1 1/2 tablespoons slivered almonds

Scrub the oranges and boil them whole for 1 1/2 to 2 hours until they are very soft. When cool, cut them up roughly and take the seeds out. Pulp them in a food processor.

Beat the eggs and fold in all the other ingredients. Pour the batter into a buttered and floured cake pan and sprinkle the top with slivered almonds. Put into an oven preheated to 425°F for about an hour. Leave to cool in the tin for 10 minutes before turning out on a wire rack.

WALNUT CAKE

Ingredients
1 cup walnuts
5 egg whites
1 1/2 cups superfine sugar
1/2 cup apricot jam

Grind the walnuts in a food processor. Beat the egg whites until they are stiff. Gradually add the sugar, then the walnuts. Divide the mixture in half and make two 7 inch rounds. Use a flan ring if you have one. Put onto a well-greased and floured baking sheet. Bake in a preheated oven at 350°F for 10 minutes.

When cool, spread the apricot jam over one layer and place the other on top. Sprinkle the top with confectioners' sugar.

FRUIT DESSERTS

PRUNES IN BRANDY

Ingredients

1 pound prunes
1 stick cinnamon
3 cloves
Peel of half an orange
1 cup superfine sugar
1/2 cup water
1/2 bottle brandy

Fill a sterilized wide-necked bottle with prunes. They should fill three-quarters of the bottle. Tuck in cinnamon, cloves and peel amongst the fruit. Make a sugar syrup by heating the sugar and water. Let it cool and pour over the fruit. Top the bottle up with brandy. Seal and label. Keep for 2 months before opening.

PLUM PUDDING

Ingredients

1 pound golden raisins
1 cup raisins

1 cup prunes, pitted
1/2 cup dates, pitted
1/2 cup currants
2 tablespoons chopped candied peel
1 cooking apple, peeled and grated
1 tablespoon grated lemon peel
1 cup brandy
1/3 cup butter

So simple to prepare are these prunes in brandy.

3/4 cup brown sugar
3 eggs
3 cups day-old breadcrumbs
2 tablespoons flour
1/2 teaspoon ground allspice berries
1/2 teaspoon grated nutmeg
1/2 teaspoon ground cinnamon
1/2 teaspoon baking soda
1/2 teaspoon salt

Chop up all the dried fruits and mixed peel, and place in a large bowl. Add the apple, lemon peel and brandy. Mix well, cover and leave for a week.

Beat the butter until fluffy: add the sugar and beat until the mixture is creamy. Add the eggs one at a time, beating well in between. Combine the cream mixture with the fruit and bread crumbs. Sift the flour, spices, soda and salt and add to the cake mixture.

Double grease heatproof basins by melting a little butter and brushing it over the entire surface of the basin, refrigerating for 10 minutes and greasing again. This will ensure the pudding will turn out perfectly. Transfer the cake mixture into the individual basins.

Cover the top of each basin with 2 layers of kitchen foil and tie with string. Place in a saucepan with boiling water halfway up the side of the basin. Steam for 6 hours. Check the water level in case you have to replace some. Keep the foil cover on and store in the refrigerator.

On Christmas Day, reheat in the same way for 2 hours.

CHERRIES IN BRANDY

Ingredients
3 pounds dark cherries, under-ripe
2/3 cup granulated sugar
1/2 cup water
1 cinnamon stick
1/2 bottle brandy

Wash the cherries and trim the stalks to within 3/4 inch of the fruit. Prick over cherries with a needle and put them in a wide-necked, sterilized jar.

Put the sugar, water and cinnamon stick into a saucepan, dissolve the sugar and simmer for 5 minutes. Pour over the cherries. Now pour the brandy over the cherries and fill up the jar. Seal and store in a cool place for at least a month before opening.

FRUIT LIQUEURS

STRAWBERRY GIN

Ingredients
4 cups strawberries
1 1/2 cups superfine sugar
1/2 to 1 bottle gin

Clean and hull the strawberries and pack into a wide-necked sterilized jar. Pour sugar over and then top the bottle up with gin. Store for 1 to 2 months or until strawberries lose their color.

   Strain liquid through cheesecloth and pour into a sterilized bottle and store for a month.

PASSIONFRUIT LIQUEUR

Ingredients
2 cups passionfruit pulp
1 cup brown sugar
1 quart white rum

Put the passionfruit in a sterilized jar. Make the syrup by putting the sugar and rum in a sauce-pan over a low heat and dissolving the sugar. Do not let it come to a boil. Pour the syrup over the fruit and seal. Do not open for at least 2 months.

PINEAPPLE LIQUEUR

Ingredients
1 pineapple, peeled and finely sliced
1 1/2 cups superfine sugar
1/2 bottle brandy

Choose a jar that will contain the pineapple, layer on layer, with about 1 inch left at the top. Put the fruit in a sterilized jar, following the original shape of the pineapple, and add the sugar. Cover well with brandy, making sure there are no air bubbles. Seal, label and store.

ORANGE LIQUEUR

Ingredients
4 oranges
2 cups superfine sugar
1 cup water
1/2 bottle brandy

Cut oranges in half and squeeze out the juice; retain. Cut the peel into bite-sized pieces and remove any pith. Make a sugar syrup by dissolving the sugar, orange juice and water then simmering for 15 minutes. Put peel into wide-necked sterilized jars and pour the syrup over. Top the bottles up with the brandy. Seal, label and store for 2 months.

Orange peel and sugar syrup transform cheap brandy into nectar fit for the gods. Serve this to ensure a very mellow ending to a successful dinner party.

QUINCE VODKA

Ingredients
2 ripe yellow quinces
1 cup superfine sugar
1/2 to 1 bottle vodka

Wash quinces and remove fluff, stalks and cores but not the skin. Cut into small pieces. Put into a wide-necked jar. Pour sugar over and top the bottle up with vodka. Seal and store for 4 months. Strain the liqueur into a sterilized bottle and seal.

Cooking

with

Cheese

LEARN ABOUT CHEESE

Cheese is one of the most varied and tantalizing of all the foods the cook has to choose from in the country kitchen. There are hundreds of different cheeses available from around the world, each with its own character, but some generalizations can be made about the main classes of cheese. Listed below are some categories of cheese that are worth knowing. The best way to gain a good knowledge of cheese available in your area is to find a specialty cheese store or good cheese section in a supermarket and ask the sales person about the cheeses.

FRESH CHEESES

These are the simplest cheeses, the closest to milk. Made from the fresh, acid-set curd (aided by a little rennet) as it is separated from the whey, these are not at all ripe. Moisture content is high and the storage life short.

Varieties include cottage cheese, cream cheese and ricotta, which is made from whey proteins. This is a popular cheese sometimes made at home; it is delicious with vegetables and fruit salads and very popular for making cheesecakes.

SOFT CHEESE

These are matured for a short time, more rennet is used to set the curd, and water content is lower than that of the fresh cheeses. The group includes a number of specialized cheeses such as, camembert and brie, which are ripened by molds; feta, a Greek cheese ripened in brine; and mozzarella, matured for only 1 month.

The best of all soft cheeses for cooking is fresh mozzarella. Older mozzarella is bland but melts into a juicy, slightly springy topping on baked pasta dishes such as lasagne al forno.

FIRM CHEESES

These comprise the largest group and include the main table cheeses: the cheddars, edam, gouda, samsoe, cheshire, Swiss and provolone. Members of the group also figure largely in cooked dishes. In flavor they can range from mild to

mature, but there are a few specially flavored fancy cheeses in this group, such as the famous blue cheeses: stilton, Danish blue, roquefort from France and gorgonzola from Italy.

HARD CHEESES
Most of the hard cheeses, which are also the driest and keep for the longest time, originated in Italy: parmesan, romano, pecorino, pepato. The hard, granular texture makes them ideal for grating.

When planning a suitable diet for your family, it is important that cheese and other dairy products are considered. As well as being nutritious, they provide interest and variety to meals. The greatest value of cheese is as a source of protein. It provides important calcium (for bone building and repair) and valuable B vitamins.

However, most of us eat cheese because we enjoy it. It is quite an adventure visiting a modern cheese store or the cheese counter at major food halls, for it is difficult choosing from the ever-growing selection our cheese-makers are producing.

COOK'S NOTES:
Serve cheese as the French do, after the main course, so that diners can finish their red wine with it. They rarely eat bread or crackers with cheese and eat it with a knife and fork. In Italy cheese is eaten alone, before dessert or fruit.

STORING CHEESE

As most cheese is bought ready to eat, the amount of a particular cheese you buy should depend on its ability to keep. Hard cheeses like parmesan, for instance, have the best keeping qualities and may be stored for several months. As with firm table varieties such as cheddar, which will keep in excellent condition for several weeks, they may be bought in large quantities.

Soft cheeses such as camembert and mozzarella will keep for a shorter period and thus should be bought in smaller amounts for more immediate use. The perishable fresh types such as cottage cheese should be used within about a week of purchase or by the 'use by' date.

Cheese should be stored in the refrigerator, although this is not essential for processed cheese.

To prevent cheese from drying out, cover it with foil or plastic wrap or put it in a plastic bag or an airtight container.

Mold sometimes develops on cheese when it is stored for long periods without being disturbed. The mold that normally grows is the harmless Penicillium kind and may be cut off. Throw the piece of cheese away if in doubt about the freshness.

A 'use by' date should appear on all cheese packs. This is a safeguard to insure that the product is the freshest available. Unopened packages of cheese may, however, still be in usable condition after that date. On the other hand, poor storage at higher temperatures than recommended will reduce the life of most dairy products quite dramatically, and a product with a specific 'use by' date may well be past its prime by then.

Always take cheese from the refrigerator in sufficient time, approximately an hour, for it to return to room temperature before being eaten. This will ensure your enjoyment of the full cheese flavor.

It is advisable not to leave cheese standing in a warm kitchen for long periods of time. If you prepare a cheese board prior to the end of a dinner or luncheon party, it should be placed in a cool area and, if necessary, covered with a damp cloth or plastic wrap.

FREEZING

Freezing is not generally recommended for cheese, but some cheeses can be successfully frozen. Cottage cheese, for example, freezes well; if anything, it becomes better textured after freezing.

Although the firm cheeses, such as mature and processed cheddar, Swiss, gouda and edam, can be frozen, their texture will become crumbly and slightly furry on the palate. Feta cheese, which normally has a crumbly body, is not significantly affected by freezing. Cream cheese, when frozen in a foil package, keeps its spreading and blending qualities for about 2 months.

For best results, freeze pre-packed cheese in its unopened original pack; to avoid deterioration of body, freeze cheese in portions of no more than 1/2 pound; freeze as soon as possible after purchase; do not freeze any product that has signs of deterioration; thaw as slowly as possible, preferably in the refrigerator.

MAKING FRESH CHEESE

Fresh cheese is a very useful food. It is high in protein and therefore important nutritionally, and there are many ways to vary the eating of it.

Cottage cheese is very easy to make at home. Ideally, unpasteurized milk should be used, but this is hard to obtain unless you live on a farm or keep your own cows or goats. It can, however, be made with pasteurized milk and even with reconstituted skimmed milk powder. The milk is left to sour and curdle. You can, if you like, add rennet. Rennet, which is made from the stomach lining of calves and also comes from some plants such as the fig and thistle, produces a digestive enzyme called rennin which effects the coagulation of milk without souring. Making the curds for cottage cheese is the same as making junket, without the sugar and flavoring. Sometimes rennet is sold in tablet form. Do not use more than the specified amount; if too much is used, it produces a metallic taste. Do not use rennet if you are on a low-salt diet.

The easiest and cheapest cheese is made with instant skimmed milk powder, which seems to sour very quickly. To make a cup of cottage cheese, make up 1 3/4 pint of skimmed milk following the directions on the packet. Use fairly warm water and set the bowl in a warm place, usually above the stove. You need a temperature of about 68°F to 70°F. Cover the bowl with a dish cloth to keep the dust off and leave it for 24 to 36 hours. Do not leave milk longer than this, for if it has not soured naturally by then, it means the milk has probably gone bad.

When it has soured properly, the curd will become firm like junket and will be surrounded by liquid which is called whey. Ladle the curd into a strainer lined with a piece of cheesecloth. The curd must be firm or else it will drain away and leave little cheese. Lift the cheesecloth up, put a clothes peg or string around the top to secure all ends, and hang it up, with a bowl underneath to catch the drips. Leave for about 24 hours. By then the curd will have become a soft creamy cheese, ready to be used in any way you wish.

The variations of cottage cheese are endless. It can be used for both sweet and savory dishes. The fresh cheese can be used in place of butter or margarine for sandwiches, with jacket potatoes, or as a cake filling if mixed with sugar. One stiffly beaten egg white folded into 8 fl oz of whipped sweetened cheese, set in heart-shaped molds and allowed to drain for an hour or so, makes the famous Coeur à la Crème, delicious with fresh strawberries

FRESH COTTAGE CHEESE

Ingredients
2 quarts milk
2 tablespoons natural yogurt
1/2 rennet tablet
1/2 teaspoon salt

Heat the milk just to room temperature, stir in the yogurt, and bring very slowly to a little above blood heat 110°F. Crush the half rennet tablet with water and stir it into the milk and yogurt mixture. A seemingly rich curd will develop on the surface. If you pull it from the sides of the saucepan you will see the thin whey that lies below. Line a strainer with a double layer of fine cheesecloth and pour in the curds. Let the drainage proceed for 4 hours or more. You will have about 4 oz of soft, creamy cheese. Add a little salt.

For a firmer cheese, press with a weight while draining. For a creamy cheese, add a tablespoon of heavy cream.

YOGURT CHEESE (LABNEH)

Ingredients
2 1/2 cups plain yogurt
2 tablespoons olive oil
2 tablespoons chopped parsley
1 teaspoon chopped, chives or mint

Place a triple layer of cheesecloth in a deep bowl, leaving the corners hanging over the edge. Spoon the yogurt into the center and gather up the ends of the cheesecloth; tie with string. Lift up this cheesecloth bag and suspend it over the bowl (this can be done by pushing the handle of a wooden spoon through the top of the bag and resting the spoon on the top edge of the bowl (if it is deep enough). Let it drip for about 5 hours, no longer. In hot weather this should be done in the refrigerator.

*Yogurt cream cheese
makes an excellent
starter stuffed into ripe
red tomatoes.*

Remove the cheesecloth and turn the cheese out onto a round plate. Make indentations all around the top and center of the cheese and sprinkle with the oil. Scatter the herbs over it and serve with thinly sliced light or dark rye bread.

YOGURT CREAM CHEESE

Ingredients
2 cups plain yogurt
1 cup cream

In a bowl combine the yogurt and cream. Pour the mixture into a strainer lined with a double thickness of dampened cheesecloth and set it over a bowl. Let the mixture drain for 0 hours or until the whey has drained off and the curds are firm. Makes about 1 1/2 cups.

WAYS TO USE YOGURT CREAM CHEESE

1 Halve a small ripe melon, remove the seeds, fill with a few spoonfuls of yogurt cream cheese and sprinkle with a little brown sugar.

2 Curl a few slices of prosciutto and serve with yogurt cream cheese to which fresh herbs have been added, and serve as a first course.

3 Cut the tops off 6 small tomatoes, scoop out the centers, and fill with yogurt cream cheese with herbs.

4 Mound about 1/2 cup yogurt cream cheese on a dessert plate, mask with sweetened very lightly whipped cream, and surround with any fresh summer fruit, or sliced and halved stewed or canned apricots, plums or peaches.

5 Offer a little black pumpernickel or Scottish oatcakes with yogurt cream cheese in place of a cheese board at the end of a meal.

CRACKER RECIPES & TEMPTING NIBBLES

1/4 cup Parmesan cheese, grated
A pinch of cayenne
A pinch of salt
2 cups flour

Beat the butter until soft and creamy; add egg yolks one at a time. Stir in the grated cheese, sift the cayenne, salt and flour into the mixture and very lightly fold in. Do not over handle the dough. Shape into a ball, wrap loosely in plastic wrap and flatten it out slightly. Chill for 2 hours.

You may need to add a little cold milk to bind the dough.

Lightly flour a work surface. Roll the dough out gently. If the edges crack, press them together, then continue gently rolling. Cut into 1/2 inch rounds. Brush with egg glaze if you like; you can also press a split almond into the top. Bake on lightly greased baking sheets in a hot oven 400°F for 8 minutes.

Cool for a few minutes on trays, then remove to a wire rack. Store in airtight containers.

Cheese sables are tasty cheese crackers that are pleasant to eat any time of the day.

CHEESE SABLES

Ingredients
3/4 cup butter
2 egg yolks

CHEESE & ALMOND BISCUITS

Ingredients

2 tablespoons sesame seeds
3/4 cup butter
1 1/2 cups Cheddar cheese, finely grated
1/4 cup Parmesan cheese, grated
1 1/2 cups flour
1 teaspoon paprika
1 teaspoon salt
Chopped walnuts or pecans or
*   slivered almonds*

Toast sesame seeds in a dry pan until golden; turn onto a plate. Cream together the butter and cheeses. Sift the flour, paprika and salt together and add to the creamed mixture with the sesame seeds. Mix well and shape the mixture into rolls about 1 1/2 inches in diameter. Wrap each roll in plastic wrap, then place the rolls in freezer bags and store in the freezer. When needed, cut rolls into thin slices about 1/8 inch thick and arrange them on a lightly greased baking sheet. Top each slice with chopped walnuts or pecans or a few slivered almonds pressed lightly into the dough.

Bake in a moderate oven 350°F for 12 to 15 minutes or until golden.

COCONUT CHEESE BISCUITS

Ingredients

4 tablespoons grated mature
*   Cheddar cheese*
4 tablespoons self-rising flour
4 tablespoons, melted butter
A pinch of cayenne
A pinch of salt
Coconut for rolling

Combine the cheese, flour, melted butter, cayenne and salt, and mix well. Roll into small balls, then toss in coconut. Place on lightly greased baking sheets and bake in a moderate oven 350°F for 15 to 20 minutes or until golden brown. Makes 12.

Roll out on a lightly floured board to about 1/4-inch thickness. Cut with a floured cookie cutter into small rounds. With a lightly floured rolling pin, roll each round very thinly and prick with a fork.

Place on baking sheets and bake in a hot oven 400°F for 8 to 10 minutes or until they are well puffed and golden.

Easing the oatcakes from the skillet. If you are on a low-cholesterol diet you could substitute cold-pressed virgin olive oil instead of suggested fats.

WATER CRACKERS

Ingredients

1 cup flour
1/2 teaspoon baking powder
A pinch of salt
2 tablespoons butter or margarine
Water

Sift flour into a bowl with baking powder and salt. Rub the butter into the flour with your fingertips until it is evenly distributed. Stir in enough water to make a firm dough.

OATCAKES

Ingredients

1/2 cup medium oatmeal
A pinch of bicarbonate of soda
A pinch of salt
2 teaspoons melted lard, bacon drippings or butter
1/2 cup hot water
Mixture of oatmeal and flour for rolling

Place the oatmeal, bicarbonate of soda and the salt in a mixing bowl and stir to combine. Make a well in the center, and pour in the melted fat and enough hot water to make a stiff paste. You might need to add a little more water. Turn out onto a work surface liberally spread with a mixture of oatmeal and flour. Roll into a ball, then pat out to a round about

1/4-inch thick. Sprinkle again with a little extra oatmeal and cut into quarters.

Place on a lightly greased hot griddle or in a heavy skillet and cook over medium heat until the underside is lightly brown and the edges curl slightly. Turn with a spatula and brown the other side. Serve warm or store in an airtight tin and broil lightly before serving.

Variation: You can also cut the flattened dough into 3-inch rounds. These oatcakes are good on the cheese board.

CHEESE BALLS

Ingredients
4 egg whites
1/2 pound Gruyère cheese, freshly grated
Fine breadcrumbs

Beat the egg whites until they are very stiff. Fold in the cheese. Make tiny balls from about a teaspoonful of the mixture, then roll them in fine breadcrumbs.

Plunge the balls into hot oil 365°F until lightly browned or golden. Drain and serve immediately.

BUBBLE BREADS

Ingredients
2 1/2 cups all-purpose flour
1 teaspoon salt
1 tablespoon butter
Milk

Sift flour and salt into a mixing bowl. Rub butter into flour and mix into a stiff dough with a little milk. Knead well, take pieces of dough and roll out very thinly on a floured surface. Cut into strips or rounds with a 2 1/2-inch diameter cutter. Place on lightly greased baking sheets. Prick with a fork, brush with milk. Bake in hot oven 425°F for 10 to 12 minutes.

It is fun to make these breads and watch them swell up in the oven. They make the perfect accompaniment to pungent cheeses.

CHEESE PUFFS

Ingredients
1 pound feta cheese
12 ounces ricotta cheese
5 eggs
1/2 cup parsley or mint, finely chopped
20 sheets filo pastry
Butter, melted

Crumble the feta cheese, add the ricotta and mix together well. Add eggs, beat thoroughly, and fold in the parsley or mint. Brush a sheet of filo with melted butter, and fold in three lengthways. Cut the folded filo into two equal portions; each will make one puff. Place one portion on a flat surface, brush with melted butter, fold in half lengthways, making a strip about 2 inches wide. Brush with butter.

Place 2 teaspoons of the cheese mixture in the bottom right-hand corner of the strip and fold the corner over to form a triangle. Continue folding to the end of the strip, making sure that you retain a triangular shape with each fold.

Brush the triangles lightly with butter and place on a baking sheet. Bake in a hot oven 400°F for 30 minutes or until golden. Makes 40.

CHEESE CRACKERS & STRAWS

Ingredients
3/4 cup flour
1/4 cup butter
3/4 cup mature Cheddar cheese, grated
1/2 teaspoon salt
A pinch of dry mustard
A pinch of cayenne
1 egg yolk
1/2 teaspoon lemon juice

Stir the flour into a mixing bowl. Cut the butter into small pieces and rub through flour with your fingertips until mixture resembles coarse breadcrumbs. Mix in the cheese, salt, mustard and cayenne. Beat egg yolk with lemon juice, add to flour mixture, mix to form a dough. (If necessary, add a little iced water; but the dough should be soft, not sticky). Wrap in plastic wrap and chill for 30 minutes or until required.

Cheese Crackers:
Roll the dough out thinly and cut into small rounds with a floured cutter. Bake in a hot oven 400°F for 5 to 7 minutes, or until crisp and golden. Makes about 36 single crackers.

If desired, when cooled, sandwich the crackers together when cooled with a little anchovy paste mixed with butter.

Cheese Straws:

Roll the dough out to a strip about 4 inches wide and trim the edges. With a 2 1/2 inch scone cutter, cut 3 rounds from the pastry and stamp out the centers, or cut with a sharp knife to make into rings. Cut the remaining pastry into 'straws'. Arrange the pastry shapes on a greased baking sheet. Bake in a hot oven 400°F for 5 to 7 minutes or until crisp and golden. Cool on a wire rack, and arrange the 'straws' in bundles pushed through the pastry rings.

BLUE CHEESE PUFFS

Ingredients

1/2 pound puff pastry, thaw if frozen
1/2 pound blue cheese (Danish blue
or Stilton)
1 egg, beaten

Roll out the pastry on a lightly floured surface to a rectangle about 12 x 10 inches. Cut in half lengthways, so you have two

pieces of pastry 12 x 5 inches. Cut the cheese into 16 thin fingers, about 2 inches long. Lay two rows of cheese, consisting of eight fingers, along the length of the pastry, leaving an equal space between each. Brush around each finger of cheese with a little water. Lay the second sheet of pastry over the top and press down well between each finger of cheese.

Cut between the cheese to make fingers about 1 1/2 inches wide and 2 1/2 inches long. Place on a baking sheet and brush with beaten egg. Chill.

Bake in a preheated hot oven 400°F for 15 to 20 minutes or until golden brown and puffed. Serve hot. Makes 18.

Blue cheese puffs are scumptious hot flaky canapés that make a perfect appetizer and party opener.

COOK'S NOTES:
When cooking with cheese, the best cheese will give you the best taste. Try not to skimp on quality.

GOUGERES BOURGUIGNONNES

Ingredients
1 1/4 cups milk
Salt and pepper
1 teaspoon grated nutmeg
3 tablespoons butter, cut into small pieces
1 cup plain flour
4 small eggs
1/2 pound Gruyère cheese,
  of which 3/4 cup is grated
  and the rest cut into
  small dice

Place milk, salt, pepper and nutmeg with the butter in a saucepan. Bring to a boil, ensuring that the butter has melted by the time the milk boils. Remove from the heat and add the sifted flour, all at once. Incorporate quickly and thoroughly with a wooden spoon and continue beating until the mixture forms a ball around the spoon and leaves the sides of the pan.

Allow to cool a minute or so before beating in the eggs, one at a time. Beat each egg fully into the mixture before proceeding with the rest.

Stir in the grated gruyère, then spoon small balls of the mixture onto a buttered baking sheet.

Put a piece of diced cheese into each puff, brush with a little beaten egg and bake in a very hot oven 425°F for 15 minutes until risen and golden. Serve hot.

OLIVE BREAD

Ingredients
1/2 pound stuffed olives
2 eggs
2 tablespoons olive oil
2 cups flour
2 teaspoons baking powder
A pinch of salt
2 teaspoons sugar
3/4 cup milk

Chop the stuffed olives coarsely. Beat the eggs until frothy and stir in the olives and oil. Sift the dry ingredients together and fold into the olive mixture with the milk. Mix gently. Pour into a greased 8 x 4-inch loaf pan.

Bake in a moderate oven 350°F for 1 hour. Turn out and cool; the bread should sound hollow when tapped with a knuckle. Serve cut in slices with soft creamy cheese.

ANCHOVY ROLLS

Ingredients

*1 4-ounce can anchovy fillets or a jar of
anchovy paste*
A little milk
16 thin slices bread
Butter and Dijon mustard
3 tablespoons grated Parmesan cheese

Soak anchovy fillets for 30 minutes in
enough milk to cover. Drain and pat with
paper towel.

Remove the crusts from the bread, butter
the slices and spread with a little Dijon
mustard. Sprinkle with cheese.

Place an anchovy fillet on each slice, or
spread with anchovy paste, and roll the
bread up. Place the rolls on a baking sheet
and dot them with butter, then bake in hot
oven 400°F for 6 to 7 minutes. Serve hot.
Serves 8.

AULD ALLIANCE

Ingredients

1/2 pound roquefort cheese
Whisky

Pound the cheese to a thick cream. Add
drop by drop as much whisky as it will
'drink' to make a firm cream. This can
be done in a food processor.

Pack into small earthenware pots and
chill in the refrigerator for 3 to 4 hours.

Serve with hot buttered toast or oatcakes.

*Olive bread looks
appealing and tastes
divine. It is well worth
the effort to make it at
home.*

Pears with stilton makes an exciting starter to a special meal. The poppy seed dressing adds a lovely texture to this rich country dish.

LIPTAUER CHEESE

Ingredients
2-3 anchovies or 1 teaspoon anchovy paste
1/2 cup butter or margarine
1 cup cottage cheese
1 small onion, grated
1 teaspoon chopped capers
1/2 teaspoon caraway seeds
1/2 teaspoon Dijon mustard
1/2 teaspoon paprika
Salt and pepper

Chop the anchovies finely or use the paste, and cream with the butter. Gradually add the cottage cheese, and when well mixed add other ingredients. The finished cheese must be piquant and savory; more seasoning, such as mustard or paprika, may be necessary. Pile up in a dish and surround with Melba toast or crackers.

PEARS WITH STILTON & POPPY SEED DRESSING

Ingredients
4 ounces Stilton cheese
5 ounces neufchâtel cheese or quark
3 ripe dessert pears
A squeeze of lemon juice
A small bunch of watercress

For the Dressing:
2 tablespoons olive oil
1 tablespoon walnut or hazelnut oil
1 tablespoon lemon juice
       or balsamic vinegar
1 tablespoon poppy seeds
Salt and pepper

Mash the two cheeses together with a fork, then beat together. Using two dessert spoons, scoop out little 'eggs' of cheese, shaping them with rounded spoons to a neat small oval. You should have 12 'eggs'. Place on foil, and refrigerate until needed.
  Make the dressing by shaking the ingredients in a screw–top jar. Just before serving, wash the pears well and cut them in two, lengthways. With a small teaspoon, scoop out the center core and pips. Place the pear halves flat side down and cut them in thin slices, starting from the rounded end. Lift the sliced pear halves, one at a time, onto serving plates, cup your hand over each half to spread out the slices, and drizzle a little lemon juice over them. Spoon the poppy seed dressing over each, place a bed of watercress on the side, and top with 2 cheese 'eggs'. Serves 6.

ENDIVE WITH HERB CHEESE

Ingredients
1/2 pound quark or neufchâtel cheese
2 tablespoons soured cream
4 tablespoons chopped chives
4 tablespoons finely chopped watercress
1 tablespoon paprika
2 tablespoons grated onion
1 teaspoon Dijon mustard
4 heads of endive
4 tablespoons finely chopped walnuts

Combine all the ingredients except the endive and walnuts; mix well. Cut off the base of the endive, break off leaves. Spread about 1 teaspoon of mixture along the center of each leaf. Coat the cheese in the chopped walnuts. Cover with plastic wrap and refrigerate until party time.

SOUPS & CHEESE

LEEK SOUP WITH FONDUE

Ingredients
2-4 leeks, depending on size
1/4 cup long-grain rice
3 cups chicken stock
Salt and pepper
1 cup Swiss or gruyère cheese, grated
1 cup white wine

Trim most of the green tops from the leeks, split in half, wash thoroughly to remove grit, cut into thin slices. Place in a saucepan with the rice and just enough water to cover. Simmer for 20 minutes, or until rice is tender.

Add the chicken stock, bring to a boil, and season with salt and pepper. Melt the cheese with the wine in the top of a double boiler or in a bowl set over simmering water.

Ladle the soup into heated bowls, and top each serving with a spoonful of the cheese mixture. Serve with crusty bread. Serves 4.

CLEAR SOUP WITH RAVIOLI

Ingredients
7 cups beef or chicken stock
1/2 cup dry white wine or vermouth
3 tablespoons tomato paste
1 bay leaf
Salt and freshly ground black pepper
24-30 ravioli [about half a 1-pound package]
Grated Parmesan cheese to serve

Place the stock, wine or vermouth, tomato paste and bay leaf in a large saucepan and blend together. Heat until the soup boils, then season with salt and pepper. Add the ravioli to the saucepan and simmer until tender, about 20 minutes.

Remove the bay leaf, and ladle soup into bowls. Sprinkle with a little Parmesan. Serves 6.

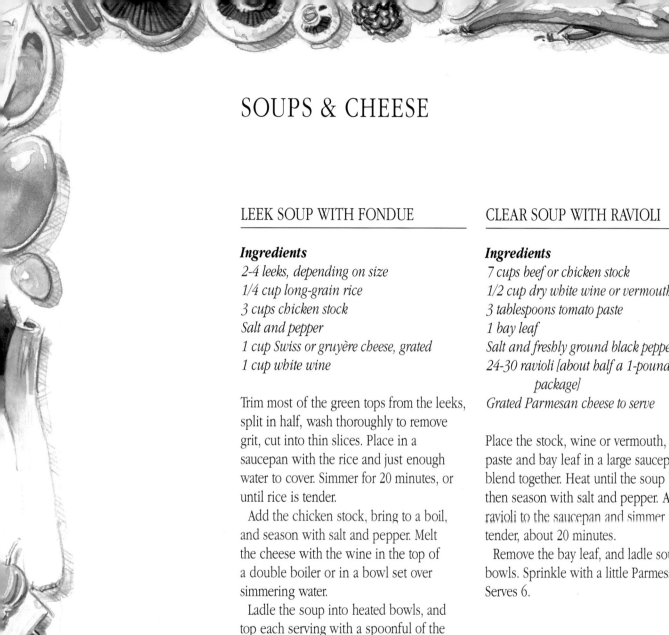

Clear soup with ravioli makes a wonderful start to a meal or a meal in itself.

STILTON SOUP

Ingredients

2 tablespoons butter
6 scallions, chopped
2 stalks celery, sliced
2 tablespoons flour
5 cups good chicken stock
Salt and pepper
1/2 cup dry white wine
6 ounces Stilton cheese, crumbled
2/3 cup light cream

Heat the butter in a medium-sized saucepan. Add spring onions and celery then cook gently for 3 to 4 minutes. Add the flour, blending well. Add stock, salt, pepper, and bring to a boil, stirring. Add the wine, and simmer gently for 15 minutes. Add the cheese and cream, stir; allowing cheese to melt. Strain through a strainer.

Serve hot with croûtons, or well chilled in summer months with cheese sables (p. 140). Serves 6.

SOUFFLES, MORNAYS & VEGETABLES WITH CHEESE

CHEESE SOUFFLE

Ingredients
3 tablespoons butter
3 tablespoons flour
1 1/2 cups milk, warmed
1/4 cup Gruyère or Emmenthal cheese,
    finely diced
1 tablespoon grated Parmesan cheese
1/2 teaspoon salt
Pepper
A pinch of cayenne
A pinch of grated nutmeg
4 egg yolks
5 egg whites
A pinch of tartrate baking powder

Butter a 5-6 cup-soufflé dish or 4 individual 1- or 1 1/2-cup soufflé dishes. Cut a double sheet of waxed paper long enough to wrap around the dish and overlap by 2 inches. It should be deep enough to extend 2 inches above the rim. Hold in position with string tied with a bow for quick removal. Place a baking sheet on a shelf in the center of the oven and set the oven to hot 400°F. Melt the butter, stir in the flour, and cook over low heat for 1 minute. Remove from the heat, cool a little, and blend in the milk, stirring until smooth. Return to the heat and stir until boiling, then take from the heat and stir in the cheese and seasonings. Beat in the egg yolks one at a time. Whisk the egg whites with the tartrate baking powder until firm, but not brittle, and fold into the cheese mixture.

Pour the mixture into the prepared dish or dishes, tap the bottom of the dish lightly on the work surface to expel any large air pockets, and smooth the top of the soufflé.

Quickly run a spoon around the top of the mixture a little in from the edge, to make the soufflé rise evenly in a crown. Immediately place the dish or dishes on the baking sheet in the center of the oven, close the door gently and turn the oven down to moderately hot 375°F. Do not open the oven door for the next 20 minutes if using one large dish.

Bake the soufflé until it is well puffed up, golden-brown on top and just firm, about

24 minutes (18 minutes for individual dishes). Have a heated serving platter ready and a warmed serving spoon and fork, and serve. Serves 4.

ASPARAGUS & CHEESE SOUFFLE OMELET

Ingredients

3 eggs, separated
Salt and pepper
1 12-ounce can asparagus stalks, drained
2 tablespoons water
1/2 cup mature Cheddar cheese, grated
2 tablespoons butter

Put egg yolks in a small bowl with salt and pepper to taste. Reserve a few asparagus stalks for garnish; roughly chop 4 or 5 stalks. Stir 1 tablespoon of water with cheese and asparagus into the egg yolks. Add more water if necessary. Whisk egg whites until very stiff, then carefully fold into the yolk mixture. Melt the butter in an 8-inch omelet pan, pour in egg mixture, and spread evenly. Cook over a low heat for 5 minutes, until the underneath is golden brown. Place pan under a preheated hot broiler for 1 minute, to lightly brown and puff top of omelet. Garnish with the reserved asparagus and serve immediately. Serves 1-2.

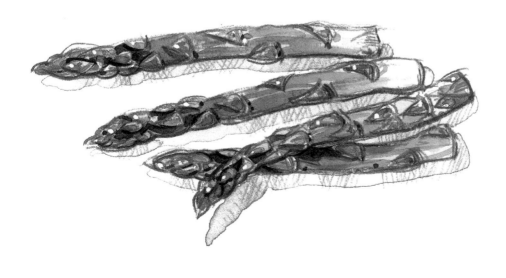

1/8 teaspoon freshly grated nutmeg
A pinch of cayenne
8 thin slices cooked ham
      or 12 slices prosciutto

Cut woody bottoms off the asparagus so that all the stalks are the same length. In a large skillet, bring to a boil enough salted water to cover the asparagus. Add the asparagus stalks and cook for about 5 minutes or longer. The cooking time will depend on individual taste.

Melt the butter in a saucepan and add flour, stirring with a wire whisk. Add the milk, stirring rapidly with a whisk. Cook, stirring, about 5 minutes until thickened and smooth. Remove from the heat. Add 3/4 cup of grated cheese, stirring rapidly with a whisk. Add egg yolk, pepper to taste, nutmeg, cayenne and beat to blend. Select an ovenproof dish large enough to hold the asparagus stalks in one slightly overlapping layer. Wrap one slice of ham compactly around each 3 stalks. Arrange asparagus in the buttered dish. Spoon the sauce all over and sprinkle with the remaining cheese.

Place the dish under a preheated broiler, cook until bubbling and golden-brown on top. Serve immediately. Serves 4-6.

Asparagus and ham mornay can be made with fresh or canned asparagus.

ASPARAGUS & HAM MORNAY

Ingredients
24 fresh asparagus stalks (about 2 pounds)
3 tablespoons butter
4 tablespoons flour
1 1/2 cups milk
1 cup cheese, grated,
      preferably gruyère or Swiss
1 egg yolk
Pepper

This is a delicious dish for a cold day and one that children of all ages like to devour.

MACARONI CHEESE

Ingredients

12 ounces macaroni
1/3 cup butter
3 tablespoons flour
2 1/2 cups milk
3/4 cup Cheddar cheese, grated
Salt and pepper
A pinch of grated nutmeg
A pinch of mustard

Bring a saucepan of salted water to boil. Add macaroni and cook for 15 minutes. Melt 1/4 cup of butter in a saucepan, stir in flour, and cook, stirring for 2 minutes. Add milk and stir until sauce boils and thickens. Beat in 1/2 cup of cheese and season with salt, pepper, nutmeg and mustard. Do not allow sauce to boil again. Drain macaroni and toss with butter. Put in a gratin dish, and spoon over sauce. Sprinkle with cheese, put under a hot broiler until cheese melts and browns. Serves 4-6.

COOK'S NOTES:
Cooking with cheese. Cooking for too long or at too high heat makes cheese tough and stringy. Grate hard cheese finely so that it will melt easily. Shred firm or soft cheese on a stainless steel grater.

MACARONI CHEESE WITH MUSHROOMS

Ingredients
1/2 pound macaroni
2 tablespoons butter or margarine
2 tablespoons flour
1 1/4 cups milk
1/2 teaspoon salt
A good pinch of pepper
1/4 teaspoon dry mustard
1 cup cheddar cheese, grated
4 ounces button mushrooms
2 tablespoons olive oil

Cook the macaroni in plenty of boiling salted water for 15 minutes. Drain. Meanwhile, melt the butter or margarine in a saucepan over moderate heat, stir in the flour, and cook gently for 1 minute. Gradually stir in the milk, beating constantly to get a smooth sauce. Bring to a boil and season well, add mustard and half the grated cheese. Stir over moderate heat until the cheese has melted.Cut the mushrooms into slices. Heat oil in a skillet and toss mushrooms lightly for 3 minutes. Add the sauce to the cooked macaroni. Pour into a hot, buttered, heat proof dish and top with mushrooms and cheese.

Place the dish under a hot broiler and cook until the cheese has melted and is a bubbling brown. Serve with hot buttered toast or a green salad. Serves 4-6.

SALMON MORNAY

Ingredients
7 ounces canned salmon
1 tablespoon butter
1 tablespoon flour
1 teaspoon dry mustard
3/4 cup milk
Salt and pepper
2 tablespoons grated Gruyère cheese
2 tablespoons fresh breadcrumbs
1 teaspoon butter

Drain salmon, remove any skin and bones, and break into chunky pieces. Melt the tablespoon of butter, blend in the flour, and cook over a gentle heat for 1 minute.

Add mustard, then the milk, stirring until the sauce thickens and is free of lumps. Season with salt and pepper. Add 1 tablespoon of grated cheese. Fold in the fish and turn into a greased ovenproof ramekin. Top with remaining cheese and breadcrumbs and dot with little pieces of butter. Place under a preheated broiler until bubbling and golden. Serves 2.

Gnocchi with butter and cheese just out from under the broiler with the cheese and butter bubbling, brown and crisp.

GNOCCHI WITH BUTTER & CHEESE

Ingredients

1 onion
1 bay leaf
3 3/4 cups milk
3/4 cup semolina or polenta
1 1/2 teaspoons salt
Pepper
2 tablespoons grated Parmesan cheese
2 tablespoons butter
1/2 teaspoon dry mustard
A pinch of nutmeg, grated
3/4 cup Gruyère cheese, grated

Peel the onion, cut it in half, and put it in a thick, heavy saucepan with the bay leaf and milk. Bring slowly to a boil, remove the onion and bay leaf, add the semolina, salt and pepper. Cook, stirring, over a low heat for 15 to 20 minutes or until very thick. Remove from the heat, stir in the grated parmesan cheese, half the butter, the mustard and nutmeg.

Spread out on an oiled baking sheet to an oblong slightly less than 1/2 inch thick. Cool. When cold, cut into squares or circles with a knife. Arrange these gnocchi, slightly overlapping, in a lightly greased shallow ovenproof dish. Sprinkle with grated gruyère cheese. Melt the remaining butter and sprinkle over the top. Bake in a moderate oven 350°F for 15 minutes, then place under a hot broiler until the top is brown and crisp. Serve while bubbling.

LASAGNE AL FORNO

Ingredients
2 onions
4 tablespoons olive oil
1 pound ground beef
1/2 pound ground pork
12 ounces fresh tomatoes, skinned
3 garlic cloves
1 teaspoon each of marjoram and basil
3/4 cup chicken or light beef stock
　　　　　(optional)
Salt and pepper
1/2 pound lasagne
4 cups milk
1 bay leaf
1/3 cup butter
3/4 cup flour
A pinch of grated nutmeg
4 cups Mozzarella, grated
3/4 cup Parmesan, freshly grated

Peel and chop the onions and soften them in the oil in a large pan. Add the meat and fry until crumbly. Roughly chop the tomatoes then peel and crush the garlic. Add the tomatoes, garlic and herbs to the pan and let them soften. If they do not make enough liquid to cook the meat in, gradually add a little stock, but always a bit less than you think you might need–you can add more later if necessary. Season with salt and pepper then cook gently in the pan for about 1 hour.

Preheat the oven to 350°F. Meanwhile cook the lasagne and leave to drain. Put milk in a small saucepan on a gentle heat and infuse the bay leaf in it for a few minutes. Make a béchamel sauce with the butter, flour and warmed milk and season it with the nutmeg, salt and pepper.

When everything is ready, put a layer of meat in a wide buttered gratin dish or casserole, then a layer of béchamel, a layer of half the mozzarella and half the parmesan, then a layer of lasagne.

Add more meat, more béchamel, more lasagne, followed by another layer of meat and béchamel, finally topping the dish with the rest of the grated cheeses.

Bake for about 45 minutes or until browned on top.

SPINACH FLORENTINE

Ingredients
1 large bunch spinach (1 1/2 pounds)
2 tablespoons butter
1 tablespoon olive oil

1 garlic clove, finely chopped
Salt
1/4 teaspoon cayenne
2/3 cup Parmesan or pecorino cheese

Wash spinach well, remove any tough white stalks, shred the leaves coarsely. Place the spinach in a large saucepan and cook, covered, for 2 to 3 minutes–toss or turn the spinach over occasionally to speed cooking. Drain well.

  Heat half the butter and olive oil in a skillet. Add garlic, salt, cayenne, spinach, and toss lightly. Place in a flameproof serving dish and sprinkle with grated cheese and remaining butter. Brown quickly under a preheated hot broiler. Serves 4.

TOAD-IN-THE-HOLE

Ingredients
1 cup flour
1/4 teaspoon salt
1 egg
1 1/4 cups milk
1 pound sausages
1 tablespoon drippings
1 cup Cheddar cheese, grated

Sift flour and salt into a bowl. Make a well in the center, add egg and milk and gradually mix to a smooth batter. Set aside for 30 minutes.

  Fry the sausages in the drippings in a flameproof dish for 5 minutes until brown on all sides. Add the cheese to the batter, pour over the sausages, and bake in a preheated hot oven 400°F for about 30 minutes. Serves 4.

Children love toad-in-the-hole, and it is an economical and easy dish to make for the family.

VEAL DISHES WITH CHEESE

VEAL BIRDS CORDON BLEU

Ingredients
6 thin veal fillets
6 thin slices ham
4 ounces Gruyère cheese,
        cut in a thick slice
2 ounces canned anchovy fillets
1/4 cup butter
1 tablespoon olive oil
Salt
1 cup stock
1 tablespoon finely chopped parsley

Beat the veal lightly with a wooden
mallet or rolling pin between two sheets
of plastic wrap to flatten. Cut into halves,
depending on how small you want
the 'birds'.

On each slice place a slice of ham, cut to
fit, a finger of cheese and a small piece of
anchovy fillet, and season with pepper.
Roll up each slice and secure with string
or small skewers.

Melt a tablespoon of the butter and the
oil in a skillet, and brown the veal rolls.

Sprinkle with salt and half the stock, and
simmer for 15 minutes. Remove to a warm
serving plate and untie the string or
remove the skewers. Then pour the
remaining stock into the pan, and simmer
for a few minutes.

Add the remaining butter with the parsley,
and shake the pan over moderate heat for
a few minutes, then pour the liquid over
veal rolls. Serves 6.

VEAL ESCALOPE

Ingredients
4 veal escalopes
Seasoned flour
1 egg, beaten
2 cups fresh breadcrumbs
1/4 cup butter
1 tablespoon olive oil
4 slices prosciutto
Parmesan cheese, roughly grated
        or shaved with a potato peeler
4 tablespoons light cream
Chopped parsley to garnish

Lay each escalope between sheets of damp waxed paper or plastic wrap and flatten them with a rolling pin until thin.

Dip the escalopes in the seasoned flour, then in egg, and finally coat with bread crumbs.

Melt the butter and oil in a skillet. When the oil is foaming, add the escalopes and cook for about 1 minute each side until golden brown.

Put the escalopes on a baking sheet. Top each with a slice of prosciutto, cover with parmesan, and pour 1 tablespoon of cream over each.

Place under a preheated hot broiler until the cheese is melted and becomes golden brown. Before serving sprinkle with parsley. Serves 4.

VEAL PARMESAN

Ingredients
4 thin veal steaks
2 eggs
4 tablespoons grated Parmesan cheese
4 tablespoons dry breadcrumbs
Oil for frying
Lemon

Place veal between 2 sheets of plastic wrap and, using a steak mallet or rolling pin, gently beat them out until they are thin. Beat eggs lightly on a plate. Spread cheese and breadcrumbs on waxed paper. Dip veal in egg, then breadcrumbs, and fry in a little hot oil for 1 1/2 minutes on each side. Serve with lemon wedges and a lightly cooked green vegetable. Serves 4.

CHEESE SNACKS

Cook bacon until crisp, then crumble. Separate the eggs, beat the yolks, then stir in the crumbled bacon and grated cheese. Whip egg whites until soft peaks form, fold through the yolk mixture. Divide among the slices of toast, covering the toast completely. Broil under a low heat for 5 minutes. Serve immediately. Serves 4.

APPLE & CHEVRE

Ingredients

1 crisp Granny Smith apple
1 teaspoon tarragon (or wine) vinegar
2 thick slices chèvre
*   or 2 small round chèvres*
Pepper
4 vine leaves, if available
2 teaspoons virgin olive oil
Sprigs of watercress
4 slices crusty French bread or oatcakes

Cut the top and bottom off the apple, then cut the apple in half to make 2 round slabs. Remove the core and seeds.

Apple and chèvre are a very harmonious combination and look attractive as well. Serve as a starter or a finish to the meal.

PUFFED EGGS & BACON

Ingredients

4 slices bacon
4 eggs
4 tablespoons grated Cheddar cheese
4 slices buttered toast

Brush the cut surfaces with vinegar. Top each piece of apple with a slice of chèvre, season with pepper, and place in an ovenproof dish on a vine leaf with another small leaf on top.

Drizzle with virgin olive oil. Preheat the oven to 400°F. Five minutes before serving, pop the dish into the oven, and cook for 4 minutes, watching that the cheese does not run too much.

Set on 2 plates, garnish with watercress, and pass the crusty bread or oatcakes. Serves 2.

DEVILED CHEESE TOASTS

Ingredients
1/2 cup mature Cheddar cheese, grated
2 teaspoons sweet pickle
A dash of Tabasco sauce
Butter
2 slices toast

Mix the cheese, pickle and Tabasco sauce together. Butter the toast lightly, and spread with cheese mixture. Place slices side by side on a buttered baking sheet.

Broil under a preheated broiler until golden brown. Serves 1.

ITALIAN FRIED SANDWICHES

Ingredients
2 teaspoons Italian mustard
8 slices bread, buttered
4 ounces Cheddar or
*   Gruyère cheese, sliced*
12 slices Italian salami
2 eggs
1 tablespoon olive oil
Salt and pepper
Oil for shallow frying

Spread the mustard evenly over the buttered side of the bread. Arrange the cheese on 4 slices, and top with the salami and remaining bread. Press firmly together.

Beat the eggs and oil together, adding salt and pepper to taste. Dip each sandwich into this mixture.

Heat the cooking oil in a skillet and fry 2 sandwiches at a time until golden brown, turning with an egg slice in order to crisp both sides. Drain on paper towels and serve.

Welsh rabbit is an old-fashioned dish that young and old continue to demand.

COOK'S NOTES:
Fromage frais is excellent in sauces where cream would normally be used. Whip the fromage frais, then add a little of the hot liquid until you have the consistency you want.

WELSH RABBIT

Ingredients
12 ounces sharp Cheddar cheese
2 tablespoons butter or margarine
1/2 cup milk or beer
1 teaspoon Worcestershire sauce
1 teaspoon dry mustard
1/2 teaspoon salt
A pinch of cayenne
1 egg
8 slices bread, toasted

Coarsely grate cheese. Melt butter or margarine in top of a double boiler over boiling water. Add milk or beer; when warm, add cheese. With a fork, stir lightly until cheese is melted. Season with

Worcestershire sauce, mustard, salt and cayenne. Remove saucepan from heat and stir in lightly beaten egg, which will cook in a few seconds. Pour over hot toast. Serve immediately. Serves 4.

INDIVIDUAL CHEESE STRATAS

Ingredients
8 square slices rye or white bread,
      trimmed to fit ramekins
Dijon mustard
1 medium onion, finely chopped
8 slices processed cheese or Cheddar
1 teaspoon salt
A pinch of cayenne
A pinch of paprika
2 tablespoons finely chopped parsley
2 eggs, beaten
2 cups milk, heated

Grease 4 individual ovenproof dishes or ramekins. Spread mustard on one side of each slice of bread. Arrange alternate layers of bread, onion and cheese in dishes, ending with cheese. Mix remaining ingredients, pour over. Put dishes in shallow pan of water and bake in a moderate oven (350°F) for 25 minutes.

PASTRY WITH CHEESE

CHEESE & HAM QUICHE

Ingredients

1 quantity rich pastry dough (right)
3-4 slices ham, cut in strips
1 1/4 cups light cream
1/2 medium onion, coarsely chopped
3 eggs
1 teaspoon Worcestershire sauce
1/2 teaspoon salt
A small pinch of cayenne
6 ounces gruyère cheese, cubed
1/4 cup parmesan cheese, grated

Roll out the dough and line an 8-9-inch pie
plate or flat ring. Chill for 15 to 20 minutes.

Place the ham over the bottom of the pie
shell. Then put the cream, onion, eggs,
Worcestershire sauce, salt and cayenne into
a bowl then beat until smooth. Add the
cubed cheese.

Pour filling into the pie shell and
sprinkle with parmesan cheese. Bake in
a moderately hot oven 375°F for 25 to 30
minutes or until the filling in the center
has set. Serves 8.

*Cheese and ham quiche
is perfect to serve at an
informal lunch party.*

MUSHROOM TARTLETS

Ingredients

1 quantity rich pastry dough
6 scallions, chopped
1/2 pound button mushrooms,
    trimmed and sliced
3 tablespoons butter
1/2 cup light cream
1 egg yolk
2 eggs
1/2 cup Gruyère cheese, grated
Salt and pepper
A tiny pinch of cayenne
A small pinch of grated nutmeg

Roll out the pastry and line 8 to 12 tartlet pans. Bake in a hot oven 400°F for 10 minutes. Flatten the centers if they puff up. Sauté the scallions and mushrooms in butter until golden, then remove from the heat. When cool, divide between the tartlet shells.

Beat the cream with egg yolk and eggs, and stir in cheese, salt and pepper, cayenne then nutmeg. Pour into tartlet shells and bake in a preheated moderate oven 350°F until filling is set and delicately browned, about 12 minutes. Makes 8-12.

RICH PASTRY DOUGH

Ingredients

1 1/2 cups flour
A pinch of salt
1/4 teaspoon baking powder
1/3 cup chilled butter, diced
1 egg yolk
2 teaspoons iced water
A squeeze of lemon juice

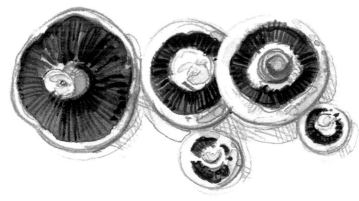

Sift the flour, salt and baking powder together. Rub in the butter until the mixture resembles coarse bread crumbs. Mix the egg yolk, iced water and lemon juice together, and stir in quickly with a knife to form a dough. Shape into a ball, wrap in plastic wrap, and chill for 20 minutes before rolling and shaping.

Chill again before baking. Should make enough dough to line a 8-9-inch flan ring or pie plate, or twelve 2-inch tartlet pans.

EASTER CHEESE & SPINACH PIE

Ingredients
2 bunches spinach or silver beet
        (about 3 pounds)
2 tablespoons olive oil
1 onion, finely chopped
12 scallions, finely chopped
Salt and pepper
1 pound feta cheese or cottage cheese,
        or a one of these cheeses
        with Cheddar
4 eggs
1/2 cup parsley, chopped
12 sheets of filo pastry
3 tablespoons butter, melted
1 tablespoon snipped dill

Trim stems off the spinach, and rinse the green leaves well. Steam just with the water still clinging to them in a tightly covered saucepan until tender. Drain well and chop finely. Press well to remove any remaining moisture.

Heat the oil in a skillet and sauté the onion until soft without coloring. Add the spinach and scallions and stir for a few minutes. Season with salt and pepper and set aside to cool.

Crumble the feta cheese into a bowl and beat in the eggs. Stir in the spinach mixture with the parsley.

Line a greased 9-10-inch deep pie dish with 6 sheets of filo, brushing each sheet with melted butter. Keep the sheets of filo under a lightly dampened dish cloth as you work. Spread the sixth layer with spinach mixture. Season the top with pepper and scatter with dill. Cover with the remaining sheets of filo, brushing each with butter as before. Press the edges firmly together and trim the excess filo, using scissors. Brush the top generously with butter.

Bake in a preheated moderate oven 350°F for 45 minutes or until the filo is golden brown. Serve hot or at room temperature.

A delicious meal for a summer lunch, tomato and cheese pie can be brought to the table in its dish.

3 tablespoons butter, softened
3 tomatoes, skinned and sliced
2 tablespoons each chopped parsley,
             basil and thyme
2 ounces Emmenthal cheese, sliced

Sift flour and salt on a work surface. Make a well in the center, add cheeses, egg yolks and butter. Gradually work into the flour. Knead until smooth, form into a ball, cover, and chill for 1 hour. Roll out the dough and use to line eight 3-inch tartlet pans or one 9-inch pan.

Chill for 20 minutes. Bake blind (lined with waxed paper and dried beans) in a preheated moderately hot oven 400°F for 20 minutes. Take out, remove the waxed paper and dried beans, and return to the oven for 5 minutes.

Layer the tomato slices in the pastry shell or shells, sprinkling each layer with herbs. Top with the cheese. Return to the oven for 5 minutes, until the cheese is bubbling. Leave to cool in the pans. Serve cool.

TOMATO & CHEESE PIES

Ingredients
1 1/2 cups flour
A pinch of salt
2/3 cups matured Cheddar cheese, grated
1 tablespoon grated Parmesan cheese
3 egg yolks

PIZZAS

TOMATO FILLING FOR PIZZAS

Ingredients
1 pound firm red tomatoes
2 garlic cloves, crushed
2 teaspoons soft brown sugar
1 tablespoon tomato paste
A sprig of oregano or basil

Peel the tomatoes and chop coarsely. Put them into a saucepan with the remaining ingredients and simmer gently, stirring occasionally for 20 to 30 minutes, until thick. Remove herb sprig before serving.

BASIC PIZZA DOUGH

Ingredients
2 1/3 cups flour
1 teaspoon salt
1 teaspoon sugar
1 sachet dried yeast
3/4 cup lukewarm water
3 tablespoons olive oil

Sift flour into a bowl with salt. Stir in sugar and yeast. Make a well in the center, add water and oil. Mix to a dough, then turn out onto a well-floured work surface. Knead lightly for 5 minutes until smooth and elastic. Put dough into a buttered bowl, turn it to coat with butter, leave to rise in a warm place, about an hour, until it has doubled in bulk.

Now turn dough out onto a floured work surface and roll into a large rectangle to fit a jelly roll pan about 14 x 10 inches or a 9-10-inch pizza pan.

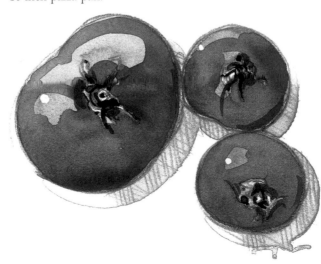

ANCHOVY PIZZA

Ingredients
1 pizza base (Basic pizza dough, p. 169)
2 tablespoons olive oil
1 small can flat anchovy fillets
1/2 quantity basic tomato filling (p. 169)
3 ounces Mozzarella cheese, thinly sliced
Black olives, pitted
Extra olive oil
1/2 cup Parmesan cheese, grated

Sprinkle the oil over the pizza base. Drain the anchovies and soak in milk for 10 minutes or so, drain and pat with a paper towel.

Meanwhile, spread the tomato filling over the dough and top with overlapping slices of mozzarella. Garnish with anchovy strips and olives. Sprinkle with extra oil and Parmesan cheese.

Bake in a very hot oven 450°F for about 18 minutes, until the crust is golden and crisp. Serve immediately.

You can omit the anchovies and use strips of dried tomatoes and pitted black olives. Serves 4-6.

PIZZA VARIETY

Select from the following garnishes:

Shrimp, black olives and capers

Anchovy fillets, black olives and mozzarella cheese

Black and green olives with pimento, shrimp, mushrooms and prosciutto

Salami strips or slices with olives, anchovy fillets and green or red peppers

Prosciutto slices with olives and mushrooms

Green and red capsicums (peppers) with anchovy fillets, olives, shrimp or salami

Capers with anchovy fillets and black olives

Sliced mushrooms with prosciutto or cured ham, olives, capsicums (peppers)

ONION & PROSCIUTTO PIZZAS

Ingredients
12 ounces puff pastry (thaw if frozen)
2 onions
1 tablespoon butter
8 slices prosciutto
1/2 cup Parmesan cheese, freshly grated
Black pepper
Chopped chives

Roll out the dough onto a floured surface, as thinly as possible. Cut out circles 3 inches in diameter (or 3-inch squares). Put them onto a baking sheet, prick very well all over with a fork, and chill for 20 minutes.

Fry the onions in the butter until soft and golden. Drain on paper towels. Trim the prosciutto, and cut into ribbon strips.

Cover the dough circles with cooked onion, sprinkle the prosciutto strips around, then the cheese, pepper and some chives. Bake in a hot oven 450°F until crisp and golden, for about 15 minutes.
Serves 4-6.

A simple and delicious onion and prosciutto pizza. Parmesan cheese and finely chopped chives are the only additions.

DESSERTS WITH CHEESE

This cheesecake is surprisingly easy to make, so do not be deterred if the instructions look complicated.

1/2 cup ground almonds
Grated peel of 1 lemon
1/2 teaspoon vanilla extract
4 eggs

DOUGH: Sift the flour into a bowl and rub in the butter until the mixture resembles fine bread crumbs.

  Add the egg yolk and enough iced water to make a firm dough. Chill for 1 hour. Roll out the dough and use it to line a greased 9-inch pie plate or springform pan. Chill for 1 hour.

FILLING: Combine the ricotta, sugar, almonds and lemon peel. Beat in the vanilla and eggs, one at a time.

  Pour into the chilled pastry shell and bake in a preheated very hot oven (425°F) for 5 minutes, then reduce the heat to moderate (350°F) and bake for a further 30 minutes or until the center of the filling is firm. Cool and chill. Serves 8.

RICOTTA CHEESECAKE

Ingredients
For the Dough:
2 cups flour
1/2 cup butter
1 egg yolk, beaten

For the Filling:
1 1/2 pounds ricotta cheese
1/2 cup superfine sugar

SEMOLINA CHEESECAKE

Ingredients

For the Dough:
1 1/2 cups flour
A pinch of salt
1/3 cup butter
1 teaspoon superfine sugar
1 egg yolk, beaten

For the Filling:
1/4 cup butter
1/2 cup superfine sugar
2 eggs, separated
Grated peel and juice of 1 lemon
1/4 cup ground almonds
1/2 pound carton fromage frais
2 tablespoons semolina
1/2 cup raisins, chopped

DOUGH: Sift flour and salt into a bowl and rub in butter until mixture resembles fine bread crumbs. Add sugar and mix to a firm dough with egg yolk. If dry, add a little water. Roll out on a lightly floured surface and line an 8-inch springform pan, pressing the pastry 1 1/2 inches up the side of the pan. Press down well to remove any air bubbles, and trim edges neatly. Chill while preparing the filling.

FILLING: Cream butter and sugar until light and fluffy. Beat egg yolks with lemon peel and juice, almonds, fromage frais, semolina and raisins. Beat egg whites until stiff, and fold in. Turn filling into pastry-lined pan and bake in a moderate oven (350°F) for 15 minutes, then a slow oven (325°F) for 55 minutes, until pastry is golden and filling is set. Remove side of pan to cool the base. Chill before serving. Serves 6-8.

LEMON & CHEESE PIE

Ingredients

For the Dough:
1 cup flour
1/4 cup butter, at room temperature
2 tablespoons superfine sugar
2 egg yolks
A few drops of vanilla extract

For the Filling:
12 ounces ricotta or cottage cheese
1 cup superfine sugar
Grated peel of 2 lemons
4 eggs
A good pinch of salt
Strained juice of 2 lemons
1 teaspoon vanilla extract

DOUGH: Sift the flour with a pinch of salt onto a work surface. Make a small well in the center, and place the remaining dough ingredients in it. Using the fingertips of one hand, work the butter, sugar, egg yolks and vanilla together to a paste; then, using a metal spatula, draw in the surrounding flour to mix and form a dough. Knead lightly until smooth, then wrap in plastic wrap and chill for an hour before using.

Roll dough out thinly and line an 8-inch flan ring with it. Trim the edges, prick the base lightly with a fork, and chill again while making the filling.

FILLING: Cream the cheese until softened, and gradually beat in the sugar until light and fluffy. Beat in lemon peel and eggs, one at a time, to prevent curdling. Next, beat in salt, lemon juice and vanilla until smooth and well blended.

Pour into the pastry shell and bake the pic in a hot oven (400°F) for 15 minutes. Reduce the heat and bake the pie in a moderately hot oven (375°F) for a further 35 minutes, or until the pastry is cooked and the filling golden. Leave the pie to cool on a wire rack and, if you like, decorate with candied lemon slices and a dusting of sifted confectioners' sugar.

CANDIED LEMON: Cut 2 or 3 lemons into fairly thin slices. Dissolve 1 1/4 cups of superfine sugar in 1/2 cup of water in a saucepan over a gentle heat, and boil for about 5 minutes. Meanwhile, blanch the lemon slices in boiling water for about 10 minutes, until tender, without breaking. Drain, dry on paper towels, and poach in the syrup for about 10 minutes or until most of the syrup has been absorbed. Arrange them, overlapping, around the pie.

BRIE FRITTERS

Ingredients
1 pound piece of brie, not too ripe
1/2 cup flour
2 eggs, beaten
1 1/2 cups dry breadcrumbs
1 tablespoon crumbled, slivered almonds
1/2-1 cup salad oil
Tart redcurrant jelly or quince paste
Fresh fruit for serving

Cut the cheese into 8 triangles of equal size and roll the cheese first in flour, then in beaten egg and finally in a mixture of bread crumbs and crumbled almonds. Repeat with a second coat. Chill well.

When ready to serve, heat the oil in a large heavy skillet, and shallow fry the fritters until they are golden-brown. Drain on a paper towel and serve immediately with a tart jam. Serves 4.

Note: Quince paste is available from some cheese stores and delicatessens.

PASHKA

Ingredients

1/2 cup unsalted butter, softened
1/2 cup superfine sugar
1 pound ricotta cheese
3 hard-cooked eggs yolks
Grated peel of 1 lemon
1/2 cup currants
1/2 cup chopped candied peel
1/2 cup blanched almonds, chopped
1/4 cup heavy cream, whipped
Candied fruits and mixed peel to decorate

Cream the butter, add the sugar gradually, then beat until light and fluffy. Push ricotta cheese and egg yolks through a fine strainer. Add to the creamed mixture with lemon peel, beating until thoroughly combined. Add currants, candied peel, almonds and, lastly, fold in the whipped

cream. If the mixture is very soft, chill until it is firm enough to shape.

Pile the mixture on a serving plate and shape into a pyramid, using a broad knife or spatula. Decorate with candied fruits and mixed peel. Chill.

Note: In Russia the letters XB (meaning Christ is risen) are outlined in candied peel on one side of the pashka, and a cross on the other.

Pashka is a really festive dish to end a special meal. There are many ways to decorate it.

SOUPS
AND
STARTERS

SOUP PREPARATION

Tomato soup is great to serve as a meal on its own with crusty bread or as a starter.

Making soup with fresh country produce is one of the most pleasurable of all the culinary processes and is only surpassed by the act of eating it. Soup is generally defined as 'a liquid food prepared by boiling, usually consisting of an extract of meat with other ingredients and seasoning'.

With a light and simple stock, great dishes were prepared by our ancestors, sometimes eaten at the beginning of a meal, as many of us do today, and sometimes at the end, as they do in China. There is a story about the wonderful Italian soup, minestrone (p. 188). During the Crusades, Genoese soldiers made a basic soup stock from meat in boiling water but asked all the peasants living in and around the city to contribute vegetables and herbs. Minestrone was born, much to the pleasure of their general, Godfrey of Bouillon.

Some soups are so big and hearty they form a meal in themselves, but there are also the relatively simple and savory preparations which, by the 18th century, became established as part of the first course on any menu. Grimod de la Regnière wrote, 'Soup is to dinner what the porch or gateway is to a building', while the famous Escoffier went on to say, 'It must not only form the first portion thereof, but it must be so devised as to convey some idea of the whole to which it belongs.'

Menu planners, when deciding upon soups and starters, carefully select those that are complementary to the main dish and do not overshadow it.

EQUIPMENT

There are benefits to owning a food processor, or blender. If you are a purist, or simply old-fashioned, a manual moulinette with three removable discs for fine, medium or coarse purées and will be your essential

piece of equipment. While the modern coffee grinder or food mill has its place, a heavy-duty pestle and mortar is excellent, if you have time, to reduce garlic, peppercorns or juniper berries to their proper consistency by old-fashioned pounding.

A variety of round and conical strainers of different-sized mesh will make life easier in the kitchen. Always have a good sized soup pot, of at least 6-quart capacity, something that will take large birds or big ham bones, and make sure it has a tight-fitting lid. A large wooden chopping board for cutting vegetables and a small cleaver for soft bones and animal carcasses will make difficult preparation easier.

COOK'S NOTES
All ovens should be preheated to the specified temperature.

Fresh herbs are used unless otherwise stated. If they are unavailable, use half the quantity of dried herbs.

Use freshly ground black pepper whenever pepper is used; add salt and pepper to taste.

Use all-purpose flour unless otherwise stated.

Extra Virgin olive oil is used whenever oil is mentioned unless otherwise stated.

A good selection of reliable kitchen tools takes the drudgery out of cooking. Here are wooden spoons, a whisk, a pestle and mortar, a stainless steel manual moulinette and a sieve.

BASIC STOCKS & SAUCES

Good basic fresh stocks are, of course, the main constituents of all soups. Their preparation is easy and the ingredients need not be expensive.

Here are some points to observe. Only use raw bones if you want to make a really clear stock with a strong flavor. Otherwise, vegetable parings, meat trimmings or left-overs and carcass bones make ideal stock material. Always use the slow simmer and not the hard-boil technique or you will end up with a murky mess. Keep the meat, bones and vegetables in large pieces in order to make a clear stock. Skim the scum off the surface constantly to clear the liquid.

BASIC STOCK

Ingredients

Meat left-overs (beef, veal, chicken,
        bacon rinds, ham bones)
Vegetables, cut up
A bouquet garni
A few black peppercorns
1/4 teaspoon salt (optional)

Put all the ingredients into a large pot, cover with cold water by two-thirds. Add salt if not using ham or bacon bones. Bring slowly to a boil, skim, half-cover the pan with the lid, reduce the heat and simmer for 2 hours or until the liquid is reduced by one-third. Strain and cool, removing any fat on top.

BASIC VEGETABLE STOCK

Ingredients

10 medium-sized carrots
5 medium-sized onions
Half a head of celery, including leaves
1 tablespoon butter
4-5 black peppercorns
1 teaspoon tomato paste
Vegetable scraps

Chop vegetables and brown in the butter in a large saucepan. Add all other ingredients and cover with water. Bring to a boil, cover saucepan with lid and simmer for 2 hours. Strain off the liquid and cool. The stock will keep in the refrigerator for a few days.

Basic stock ingredients: fish bones and heads, vegetables of all types, chicken meat, solid deep cooking pots, oils and vinegars. Stock pot ingredients are wide and varied and can be made up of yesterday's left-overs.

BASIC CHICKEN STOCK

Ingredients

3 pounds chicken carcasses
3 1/2 quarts water
4 celery stalks, coarsely chopped
6 carrots, unpeeled, thickly sliced
2 brown onions, quartered
8 black peppercorns

Put the chicken pieces in a soup pot and rinse with hot water. Drain and add the cold water along with the other ingredients. Bring to a boil and simmer for 4 hours. Skim and discard froth that forms when the pot first begins to simmer. The stock will seem rather tasteless, as it has no salt. This is added when you use stock in preparation of soups and other dishes. Strain, cool and remove fat.

BASIC FISH STOCK

Ingredients

3 pounds fish trimmings, bones, skin,
head of snapper or sole
1 large brown onion, sliced
1 medium-sized carrot, cleaned and sliced
1 small stalk celery
White part of 1 leek, cleaned and sliced
10 black peppercorns
2 teaspoons white wine vinegar
1 cup dry white wine

Combine the fish trimmings and all other ingredients in a large saucepan and cover with water. Bring to a boil and skim off any froth from the top. Lower the heat and simmer, covered, for 30 minutes.

Do not overboil the fish bones, as this will produce a gluey stock. Strain through a cheesecloth-lined strainer. Return the strained stock to the pot and simmer once more, reducing it to the required consistency. Add salt to taste.

BASIC WHITE STOCK

Ingredients

3 pounds veal bones
2 onions, quartered
2 carrots, quartered
1 stalk celery, sliced
A bouquet garni
6 black peppercorns
1/2 teaspoon salt

Find the largest pot you can, 7-quarts ideally. Put the bones in and cover by two-thirds with water. Bring to a boil, skimming all the time. With the water still bubbling, add the rest of the ingredients, lower the heat and simmer for about 4 hours. Strain, cool and remove fat.

BASIC TOMATO SAUCE

Ingredients
2 x 14-ounce cans Italian tomatoes
3 tablespoons olive oil
1 teaspoon superfine sugar
1/2 teaspoon salt
1/4 teaspoon pepper
24 fresh basil leaves

Chop the tomatoes into very small pieces, or crush them with your hand, and place them in a saucepan with the juices from the opened cans. Add all the other ingredients except the basil, stir well and cook over a medium heat for about 10 minutes. Tear up the basil leaves, add them to the tomato mixture and cook for a further 10 minutes.

HOMEMADE MAYONNAISE

Ingredients
2 eggs at room temperature
1 teaspoon dry mustard
1 teaspoon salt
1 teaspoon superfine sugar
1/4 teaspoon cayenne
1 cup oil
1 tablespoon white vinegar
1 tablespoon lemon juice

Place the eggs and the dry ingredients in a food processor or blender and blend for 5 seconds. Then, with the machine still running, very gradually add the oil in a thin, steady stream until the mixture is thick and creamy. Add the vinegar and lemon juice and blend once more. Makes 11/2 cups.

VEGETABLE SOUPS

OLD-FASHIONED CREAM-OF-TOMATO SOUP

Ingredients
1 small brown onion, finely chopped
2 tablespoons butter
1/4 cup flour
1 cup milk
5 cups fresh tomatoes, peeled and chopped
1 teaspoon thyme leaves
5 basil leaves, chopped
Salt and pepper
1 cup light cream

In a large saucepan, sauté the onion in the butter for 2 minutes, then add the flour, stir and cook a further 2 minutes. Whisk in the milk, constantly until the mixture thickens. Add the tomatoes and their juices and simmer for 10 minutes. Turn the mixture into a food processor fitted with the metal blade and blend until quite smooth. Return the soup to the pan, add the herbs, season to taste and stir in the cream. Heat through but do not boil. Serves 4-6.

PEA & CUCUMBER SOUP

Ingredients

1/2 pound precooked or frozen peas
1 large potato, sliced
1/2 spanish (red) onion, sliced
4 cups basic chicken stock (p. 181)
2 tablespoons butter
1/2 cup water
1 cucumber, peeled and seeded
2/3 cup light cream
2 egg yolks, lightly beaten
Salt and pepper
Sprigs of mint

Combine peas, potato and onion in a saucepan, add 11/2 cups of chicken stock and half the butter. Simmer for 20 minutes until the vegetables are tender. Cool, transfer to a food processor, add water and blend until smooth.

  Cut cucumber into matchsticks and cook in remaining butter until tender. Add cream and beaten egg yolk to vegetable purée and blend. Heat rest of chicken stock, stir in the purée and cook over a low heat until the soup is smooth and thick; do not boil or the egg yolks will curdle. Season to taste and add the cucumber matchsticks. Serve with mint sprigs. Serves 4-6.

COUNTRY GARDEN VEGETABLE SOUP

Ingredients

1 large soup bone with meat
1 pound chuck steak, cut to 2-inch cubes
2 tablespoons oil
2 1/2 quarts water
1 bay leaf
4 black peppercorns
1/3 cup pearl barley
1 medium-sized brown onion, chopped
2 cups mixed vegetables (sliced carrots,
        chopped celery, peas, corn)
3 cups ripe tomatoes, chopped
1/2 teaspoon each chopped rosemary,
        thyme and marjoram
1/2 teaspoon salt
Pepper

In a large soup pot, brown soup bone and chuck steak in oil on a medium heat, turning gently. Add water, bay leaf and peppercorns. Lower heat, cover and simmer for 2 hours. Remove bone, skim the fat off the liquid, add barley and simmer for a further 45 minutes. Add vegetables and herbs. Simmer, covered, for 25 minutes or until vegetables are tender. Season. Remove bay leaf before serving. Serves 10-12.

Opposite page:
Old-fashioned cream-of-tomato soup. It is eaten either hot in winter or cold in summer and is just as good either way.

COUNTRY PUMPKIN SOUP

Ingredients

*1 pound pumpkin, peeled and cut
    into pieces*
1 brown onion, sliced
1 1/2 quarts water
1/2 teaspoon salt
2/3 cup orange juice
2/3 cup light cream
2 teaspoons curry powder

Put the pumpkin, onion and salt into a soup pot with the water. Cover and boil for 15 minutes or until pumpkin is soft. Drain, reserving the liquid, and purée the pumpkin and onion in a food processor fixed with the steel blade. Add 2/3 cup of the reserved cooking liquid, together with the orange juice, cream and curry powder. Purée the mixture in the food processor again until it is quite smooth.

Refrigerate and serve cold. If you prefer your soup hot, reheat it gradually in a saucepan, but do not boil. Serves 4.

VICHYSSOISE

Ingredients

4 leeks, washed and sliced
4 cups potatoes, chopped
1 1/2 quarts basic chicken stock (p. 181)
2 tablespoons butter
1/4 teaspoon paprika
A pinch of grated nutmeg
1/4 teaspoon pepper
A pinch of cayenne
Salt
1 cup milk
1/2 cup light cream
1 tablespoon chopped chives

In a large saucepan, sauté the leeks and potatoes in butter. Add the chicken stock and other spices, season to taste and simmer the vegetables for 40 minutes or until tender. Blend the vegetables and liquid in a food processor fitted with the steel blade and pour back into the saucepan.

Add the milk and cream and simmer gently until heated through.

Chill and serve sprinkled with chopped chives. Serves 6.

Beets makes one of the best of all the thick soups and their wonderful burgundy shade complements the rosé wine you will want to drink with it.

BEET SOUP

Ingredients

2 leeks, washed
1 pound potatoes, quartered
5 cups basic white stock (p. 182)
1 large beet, peeled and cut into chunks
4 tablespoons butter
1/3 cup light cream

Slice the white part of the leeks, discarding the rest, and cook gently in 1 tablespoon of butter until soft but not brownish. Add the potatoes and stock to the leeks and simmer until the potatoes are tender. Blend the mixture in a food processor until smooth, then return it to the washed saucepan. Bake the beet in a moderate oven (350°F) with a tablespoon of butter until tender, purée in the blender and add to the potato. Mix well together over a low heat and dilute with a little stock if the soup is too thick. Stir in the rest of the butter and cream just before serving. Serves 4-6.

COOK'S NOTES:
Leeks are often full of mud. Clean them by cutting off the roots, halving the vegetable lengthwise, removing outer tough coat and separating remaining layers in a sink full of cold water.

OLD-FASHIONED SPLIT PEA SOUP

Split peas are peas that have been dried until
they split into two parts. Either yellow or
green peas can be used in this soup.

Ingredients
2 cups split peas
2 1/2 quarts boiling water
1 pound ham hock
1 large brown onion, chopped
1 medium-sized carrot, diced
1/4 teaspoon pepper
Salt

Wash and pick over the peas, then place
them in a deep pot with boiling water. Add
the ham hock, onion, carrot and pepper then
simmer, covered, for 1-1 1/2 hours until the
vegetables are very soft. Remove the ham
hock, dice the meat and return to the pot,
discarding the bone.
    Skim any excess fat off the soup and
season to taste. Serve with toasted croûtons.
Serves 8.

MINESTRONE

Ingredients
1/2 pound dried haricot or kidney beans
1/2 pound salt pork, diced
2 garlic cloves, finely chopped
1 Spanish onion, quartered
2 1/2 quarts white stock (p. 182)
4 carrots, finely sliced
4 celery stalks, finely sliced
1/2 small cabbage, sliced
4 large ripe tomatoes, chopped
3 cups green beans, cut into 1-inch lengths
1 1/2 cups green peas, shelled
2 cups macaroni, broken to 2-inch lengths
1/4 teaspoon pepper
Salt
2 tablespoons chopped parsley
2 tablespoons olive oil
4 tablespoons grated Parmesan cheese

Soak the dried beans overnight; drain and
put in a pan of unsalted water. Boil rapidly
for 10 minutes, then simmer until just tender.
Sauté the salt pork in a skillet until golden,
add garlic and onion and cook until just
soft. Add the stock and all the other
vegetables except the peas. Bring to a boil,
then simmer gently, covered, for an hour.

Twenty minutes before serving, add the peas and macaroni, bring back to a boil and simmer until the macaroni is tender.

Adjust the thickness of the soup by adding a little water, if liked. Season with salt and pepper and, at the last minute, add the parsley and olive oil. Serve hot, sprinkled with grated Parmesan. Serves 8.

SPLIT PEA & CUMIN SOUP

Ingredients
1 pound split peas
4 cups water
1 large brown onion, chopped
2 teaspoons olive oil
2 teaspoons ground coriander
2 teaspoons ground cumin
1 medium-sized carrot, chopped
1 pound pumpkin, peeled, seeded
*   and chopped*
1 cup cauliflower, chopped
4 cups basic vegetable stock (p 180)
Pepper
1 tablespoon low-salt soy sauce
Chopped parsley

Put the peas in a saucepan and cover with the water. Boil with lid off and skim foam off the top. Cook over a medium-high heat for 10 minutes, then drain. In a medium-sized saucepan, cook the onion in the oil for 2 minutes, add the coriander and cumin and continue to cook for a further 2 minutes, stirring constantly. Add chopped vegetables and stock and bring mixture to a boil, stirring occasionally. Reduce heat and simmer, covered for 30 minutes. Season with pepper and soy sauce and serve hot sprinkled with the chopped parsley. Serves 4.

Minestrone is made from a large selection of vegetables and pasta. It is a meal in itself, and may include dried beans, carrots, cabbage, tomatoes, garlic, peas, fresh beans and celery.

Cut the leeks into 2-inch pieces, combine with the onion and sauté in the butter over a low heat until the vegetables are soft. Transfer to a large soup pot and add the rest of the ingredients. Bring to a boil, then lower the heat and simmer for 30 minutes or until the cabbage is tender. Season to taste and serve very hot. Serves 6.

VEGETABLE SOUP WITH GINGER

Ingredients
4 cups basic chicken or vegetable
stock (p 180-1)
5 ounces fresh ginger root, peeled
1/2 small cauliflower, cut into small florets
2 carrots, cut into julienne strips
2 celery stalks, chopped
1 leek, cleaned and chopped
Salt and pepper
4 tablespoons light cream
Ground ginger

Place stock and ginger root in a large saucepan and cook until ginger is very tender. Remove ginger, rub it through a strainer and return it to the stock with all the other vegetables. Season to taste and simmer until the vegetables are just tender.

Old English cabbage soup, a plain, tasty and very economical soup.

OLD ENGLISH CABBAGE SOUP

Ingredients
2 leeks, washed
1 large brown onion, finely chopped
2 tablespoons butter
5 cups bush chicken stock (p 181)
1 small cabbage, cored and cut
into 8 wedges
A good pinch of ground cloves
1/8 teaspoon crushed saffron threads
A pinch of mace
1/2 teaspoon salt
1/4 teaspoon pepper

Just before serving add the cream. Ground ginger may be sprinkled over the top as a garnish. Serves 4-6.

CREAM OF PARSLEY SOUP

Ingredients
2 cups parsley
1 large brown onion, sliced
1 1/2 cups celery, washed and sliced into
*   small pieces*
2 tablespoons butter or margarine
3 tablespoons flour
2 quarts basic chicken stock (p 181)
Salt and pepper
1/2 cup light cream
Extra sprigs of parsley

Wash the parsley and drain off excess water. Chop roughly and add to the sliced onion and celery. In a large soup pot, melt the butter and add the vegetables. Cover the pot and cook vegetables over a medium heat until quite soft, approximately 10 minutes. Stir in the flour to make a smooth paste, then add the stock and season to taste.

Bring the mixture to boiling point, then cover the pot, lower the heat and simmer for 25-30 minutes. Allow to cool and then purée in a food processor. Keep chilled in the refrigerator.

To serve, reheat and swirl in the cream, garnish with parsley sprigs, and have warm crusty French bread ready as an accompaniment. Serves 8.

Cream of parsley soup. The most commonly used of all the green herbs produces one of the most delicious soups.

CURRIED PARSNIP & ORANGE SOUP

Ingredients

2 tablespoons butter or margarine
2 medium-sized parsnips, thinly sliced
1 medium-sized brown onion, chopped
1 garlic clove, crushed
1 teaspoon curry powder
1 teaspoon ground cumin
1 tablespoon flour
5 cups basic chicken stock (p 181)
Finely grated peel and juice of
    2 large oranges
Salt and pepper to taste
1/2 cup light cream

Melt the butter in a large saucepan and fry the parsnips and onion until soft, about 10 minutes. Keep lid on and shake the saucepan throughout. Add the garlic and the spices and cook, uncovered, for a further 2 minutes. Stirring, add flour and cook for a further 2 minutes. Pour in stock and orange juice, bring to a boil and season to taste. Lower the heat, cover the pot and simmer for approximately 20 minutes, then allow mixture to cool. Blend until smooth in a food processor and refrigerate for 12 hours. To serve, reheat the soup, stir in half the cream and heat through without boiling. In soup bowls, swirl with remaining cream and sprinkle with grated orange peel. Serves 4.

SUMMER SWEET PEPPER SOUP

Ingredients

4 tablespoons chopped cilantro
2 sweet red peppers
1 small onion, sliced
1 cup ripe tomatoes, sliced
4 cups vegetable stock (p. 180)
2/3 cup milk
1/2 teaspoon salt
Pepper

Spread chopped cilantro across an ice-cube tray, top up with water and freeze. Cut stem end off from sweet peppers, remove seeds and slice into strips. In a large pot, combine sweet peppers, onion, tomatoes and stock. Bring to a boil, lower the heat, cover and simmer until the vegetables are tender, about 15 minutes. Drain the liquid into another pot and purée the vegetables in a food processor. Re-combine the liquid and purée, add the milk and season to taste. Refrigerate for at least 3 hours. Add cilantro ice-cubes to soup bowls when ready to serve. Serves 4.

Summer sweet pepper soup. An unusual summer soup made all the more intriguing by floating cilantro ice cubes.

COOK'S NOTES:
The fresh cilantro herb is not the same as the coriander spice used in Indian cookery, which comes in powdered form or as whole seeds. The herb and the spice are not interchangeable in recipes.

ICED LEMON SOUP

Ingredients
1/2 lemon peel, finely grated
4 egg yolks
Juice of 2 lemons
2/3 cup sour cream
2 1/2 cups basic white stock (p. 182)
2/3 cup light cream
Chives, chopped

Combine the lemon peel with the egg yolks and beat well. Blend in the lemon juice and the sour cream. Heat the stock and gradually add to the egg yolks, stirring constantly. Cook over a very low heat or use a double boiler and stir until the mixture thickens to a thin custard consistency. Remove from the heat source, season with salt and pepper, leave to cool, and stir occasionally.

Serve well chilled, garnished with chopped chives. Serves 4.

COOK'S NOTES:
Chilled soup is the perfect starter for lunch or dinner on a hot summer's day.

FISH-BASED SOUPS

COOK'S NOTES:
The edible part of an
asparagus stalk will
break where it is tender.
Hold the bottom end
with one hand and the
tip with the other hand,
and gently bend. Save
the broken-off ends for
soup stocks.

SMOKED FISH SOUP

Ingredients

1 1/2 pounds smoked fish fillets
1 brown onion, thinly sliced and
separated into rings
3 cups milk
2 medium potatoes, cooked and mashed
2 bay leaves
A pinch of grated nutmeg
White pepper
2/3 cup light cream
1 tablespoon chopped parsley

Put smoked fish fillets into a greased baking
dish and top with the onion rings. Pour over
just enough water to cover the fish, cover the
dish with foil and bake in a preheated oven
(350°F) for 20 minutes or until the fish is
tender. Drain and reserve the liquid,
discarding the onion. Remove the skin and
any bones from the fish and flake the flesh.

In another saucepan combine the milk and
mashed potatoes, stirring continually over
low heat until the mixture comes to a boil
and has a creamy smooth texture.

Add the reserved fish cooking liquid and bay
leaves and simmer for 5 minutes.

Remove the bay leaves, add the fish, season
with nutmeg and pepper, add the cream and
heat through.

Sprinkle the chopped parsley over the
bowls of soup just before serving.
Serves 4.

EGG & LEMON SOUP
(SOUPA AVGOLÉMONO)

Ingredients

2 quarts basic fish stock (p 182)
1/3 cup long-grain rice
3 eggs, well beaten
Juice of 2 lemons
Salt and pepper

In a large saucepan, bring the stock to a boil
and throw in the rice. Add lemon juice and a
tablespoon of cold water to the beaten eggs
and whisk till frothy.

Take a ladleful of hot stock and add it
slowly to the egg and lemon, whisking all

the time. Add a second; then a third ladleful of the stock, then pour it all back into the pot and stir well, away from the heat source.

Season with salt and pepper to taste. Do not let the soup boil once the egg and lemon juice have been added, or it will curdle. Serves 6.

Variation: If you want a creamy soup, leave out the rice and thicken the stock with a little flour mixed to a paste with cold water. Make sure you do this before combining the stock with the egg and lemon juice.

SIMPLE SEAFOOD BISQUE

Ingredients
1 pound ripe tomatoes, peeled
and chopped
2 brown onions, diced
5 cups cold water
1 teaspoon lemon juice
Salt and pepper
1 pound white fish fillets, cut into cubes
2/3 cup light cream
2 tablespoons dill, finely chopped
4 ounces small cooked shrimp, shelled

In a large saucepan, combine the tomatoes, onions, water and lemon juice and season with salt and pepper. Bring to a boil, then lower the heat and simmer for 20 minutes. Add the fish cubes to the soup and cook until they are just tender but not falling apart. Stir in the cream, check the seasoning and add the dill and the shrimp. To serve, reheat very gently if necessary. Serves 4-6.

Simple seafood bisque. The rosy pink tomato soup base sets off the shrimp as they float to the top of this great seafood soup.

VEGETABLE STARTERS

Pizza boats with ratatouille filling are scrumptious, brimming with vegetables, and smelling of herbs.

PIZZA BOATS WITH RATATOUILLE FILLING

Ingredients

For the Dough:
1 1/2 cups all-purpose flour
1 1/2 cups self-rising flour

1 tablespoon olive oil
2 eggs
1/2 teaspoon salt
5 tablespoons warm water

For the Filling:
1 medium-sized eggplant
1 cup olive oil
1 large onion, peeled and diced
1 large red sweet pepper, seeded
*   and chopped*
2 garlic cloves, finely chopped
2 cups basic tomato sauce (page 183)
1 tablespoon chopped herbs (oregano,
*   parsley, basil)*
1/4 teaspoon ground coriander
Salt and pepper
4 slices of salami
Freshly grated Parmesan cheese

Sift flours into a large mixing bowl and make a well in the center. Place oil, eggs and salt in the well and gradually combine with the flour until all the dough ingredients are well mixed. Your hands are the best kitchen implement for this process. Add water a tablespoon at a time to make a firm, smooth paste. Knead well for several minutes, then rest the dough, covered with a cloth, before rolling. A hand-cranked rolling and cutting pasta machine is ideal if you have one. Roll the dough into sheets approximately 1/8-inch thick, then cut into small oval boat shapes 2 1/2-inches long. Line the molds with the dough shapes.

Meanwhile, prepare the filling by slicing the eggplant in half lengthwise, then into strips 3/4-inch thick. Cut strips in half across the middle. Heat olive oil in a pan and cook the eggplant until soft and just turning brown. Remove from the oil and drain on paper towels. Put the onion and sweet pepper into the oil in the pan and cook until soft. Put the eggplant back into the pan with the onion mixture. Add the garlic, basic tomato sauce, herbs, ground coriander, salt and pepper. Stir gently so as not to break the eggplant, and cook the mixture for another 15 minutes on medium heat.

When the ratatouille mixture cools, fill the pizza dough boats, making sure a large piece of dark eggplant skin faces uppermost. Decorate the tops with thin strips of salami or sprinkle a little grated Parmesan cheese. Place in a preheated oven at 375°F and cook for 15-20 minutes.

CAULIFLOWER & CHEESE SOUFFLE WITH BACON

Ingredients

1 tablespoon fine breadcrumbs, toasted
1/2 small cauliflower
1 1/2 tablespoons butter
2 bacon slices, finely chopped
1 small onion, chopped
1 tablespoon flour
1/3 cup milk
2 eggs, separated
2 tablespoons grated rat-trap cheese
1 tablespoon grated Parmesan cheese
2 extra teaspoons grated Parmesan cheese
2 extra teaspoons grated rat-trap cheese

Take four 1/2-cup soufflé dishes. Grease insides, sprinkle with breadcrumbs and place on a baking sheet. Steam or boil the cauliflower until tender, drain, then blend it in a food processor until smooth. In a small saucepan, melt 1/2 tablespoon of the butter and add the bacon and onion. Stir over a medium heat until the onion is soft, about 2 minutes, and drain.

Melt the remaining tablespoon of butter in a saucepan, add the flour and stir over medium heat for 1 minute. Remove from the heat and gradually stir in the milk. Stir over

COOK'S NOTES:
Avoid bulky eggplants, the smaller ones are much more tasty.

COOK'S NOTES:
To roast sweet peppers, place under a broiler till the skin blisters all over. Cover with a cloth and allow them to cool in their own steam.

high heat until the mixture boils and thickens. Cool slightly, stir in the egg yolks, cheeses, cauliflower and bacon-onion mixture. Beat the egg whites separately until firm peaks form, then fold through the cauliflower mixture.

Pour into the prepared soufflé dishes, sprinkling the combined extra cheeses on top. Bake in a preheated oven (360°F) for 20 minutes or until puffed and browned. Serves 4.

BEAN & OLIVE SALAD

Ingredients
1 1/2 cup shelled beans
1/2 cup olive oil
Grated peel and juice of 1 lemon
2 garlic cloves, crushed
Salt and pepper
5 large black olives
2 tablespoons chopped mixed herbs
        (chives, basil, marjoram)
4 large firm tomatoes

Shell, then wash the beans and place them in a pot with plenty of water. Bring to a boil, then lower the heat and half-cover with a lid to allow steam to escape. Simmer until

tender. Drain and transfer the beans to a bowl; add oil, lemon juice and peel, garlic and seasoning to taste. Mix well, cover and leave for about 4 hours.

When almost ready to serve, pit the olives and chop them into rough pieces. Combine with the herbs and add to the beans. Slice the tomatoes thinly, arrange on serving plates, season and mound the bean mixture on top. Best served chilled. Serves 4.

ASPARAGUS & OYSTER MUSHROOMS

Ingredients
Asparagus stalks, 5 for each person
2 tablespoons butter
7 ounces white oyster mushrooms
Juice of 1/2 lemon
Salt and pepper

Clean asparagus and leave it whole. Bring a pot of water to a boil and blanch the asparagus for 4-5 minutes. Meanwhile melt the butter in a skillet and cook the mushrooms until they begin to turn brown and have a nutty aroma, about 3 minutes. Drain the asparagus and arrange it in overlapping rows with the mushrooms on individual serving plates. Add lemon juice to the butter in the skillet, season and add a little more butter if needed. Reheat lemon-and-butter mixture and immediately pour it over the asparagus.

ROASTED SWEET PEPPER SALAD

Ingredients
3 medium-sized red sweet peppers
3 medium-sized yellow or green
sweet peppers
3/4 cup capers
1 7-ounce can anchovies, chopped
A bunch of oregano, chopped
Olive oil

Skin and clean sweet peppers using roasting method, cut into strips lengthwise, each about 1/8-inch wide. In a shallow bowl lay a diagonal row of red sweet pepper strips approx. 2-inches apart. Sprinkle with capers, chopped anchovy and oregano. Repeat the process with strips of yellow peppers, in between the red strips. When all sweet peppers have been used, season with pepper and drizzle olive oil over until all are coated with oil. Cover and place in the refrigerator until the next day. Serves 6-8.

MARINATED MUSHROOMS

Ingredients
1 pound small button mushrooms
3 tablespoons wine vinegar
1/2 cup sunflower oil
1/4 teaspoon dry mustard
1/2 teaspoon brown sugar
Salt and pepper
A small bunch of parsley, chopped

Asparagus with oyster mushrooms is a unique blend of a vegetable with fungi to delight the palate.

Wipe mushrooms clean and trim stems. Any large mushrooms should be halved or quartered; leave others whole. In a bowl, whisk together the vinegar, oil, mustard and sugar. Season to taste. Add mushrooms and stir until fully coated with the marinade. Cover and refrigerate for at least 8 hours. Stir the marinade occasionally. When ready to serve adjust the seasoning. Set on individual plates and sprinkle with parsley. Serves 6.

STEAMED BUTTON MUSHROOMS WITH PORK FILLING

Ingredients
1/2 pound button mushrooms
1/2 pound ground lean pork
6 water chestnuts, finely chopped
1 tablespoon cornstarch
1 tablespoon light soy sauce
1/2 teaspoon salt
1 teaspoon finely grated ginger root
2 teaspoons cilantro, chopped
1/2 teaspoon brown sugar
Sesame oil

Wipe mushrooms with a damp cloth, but do not peel. Carefully remove stems with a little twist of the fingers, leaving mushroom caps

whole and intact. Place all the other ingredients except oil into a bowl and mix thoroughly. Fill each cap with about a teaspoon of mixture, making sure it is tightly packed and rounded on top.

Grease a heatproof dish with sesame oil and arrange the mushrooms inside. Cover the dish tightly with foil and steam the mushrooms for about 30 minutes. Drain off any excess liquid, allow to cool. Serves 4.

BASIL & RICE SALAD

Ingredients
2 cups long-grain rice
4 cups water
1 cup basil leaves, chopped
1/2 cup olive oil
1/4 cup lemon juice
1 chili, chopped
1/3 cup slivered almonds
3 garlic cloves, chopped
Salt and pepper
1/3 cup chives, chopped

Steam the rice first. I find the easiest way to cook rice is by the absorption method. Wash the rice and leave it to soak in water for 30 minutes. Drain the rice and put it in a saucepan with 4 cups of water. Bring quickly to a boil, then turn the heat down very low. Cover tightly and leave for about 20 minutes. Fluff up the rice with a fork.

Meanwhile put the basil leaves, oil, lemon juice, chili, almonds, garlic, salt and pepper into the food processor and blend to a purée. Spread rice out so it cools down quickly and doesn't stick together. When it has stopped steaming, combine the rice, basil purée and chives in a salad bowl.

Variation: Mint, parsley and other combinations of herbs are also excellent in a salad made this way.

LEEKS & JUNIPER BERRIES

Ingredients
1 tablespoon whole juniper berries
3 tablespoons olive oil
3 cups leeks, cleaned and cut
1/2 cup chicken stock
Salt and pepper

Crush the juniper berries with a pestle and mortar or coarsely grind them in a small electric blender. Sauté the crushed berries in the oil for a moment. Add the leeks and sauté, uncovered, for 2 minutes. Add the stock, cover and simmer until tender. Add salt and pepper to taste. Serves 4.

HOME-MARINATED OLIVES

Ingredients
7 ounces large black olives
2 sprigs of rosemary
2 sprigs of thyme
2 sprigs of winter or summer savory
3 small dried hot chilies (optional)
2 garlic cloves, cut into slivers
1/2 cup oil
4 basil leaves
5 sage leaves

Place olives in a bowl, fill it three-quarters full. Chop and mix together rosemary, thyme, savory and chilies (if you want a hot, spice taste). Add garlic and combine with the olives, making sure that they are thoroughly coated. Drizzle olive oil over until olives are almost covered. Arrange the basil and sage leaves as a decorative centerpiece in the bowl. It is best to prepare the marinade at least a day before use.

COOK'S NOTES:
Olive oil or other vegetable cooking oils are much less likely to be absorbed by the food you are cooking if they are fresh and clean.

Summer Melon Mint.
Pyramids of multicolored
melon balls provide a
spectacular start to any
meal. They go well after
it, too.

SUMMER MELON MINT

Ingredients
1/2 small watermelon
1 musk melon
1 honeydew melon
1/4 cup fresh lime juice
2 tablespoons finely chopped mint

Scoop watermelon into balls, removing seeds where possible. Scoop the other melons into balls or cut into decorative shapes if you have a variety of small cutters available. Place all the fruit into a bowl, pour the lime juice and chopped mint over, cover and refrigerate for at least 2 hours before serving. Serves 8.

INDIVIDUAL AVOCADO MOUSSES

Ingredients
4 ripe avocados
2 white onions, grated
1 egg, hard-cooked and chopped
2 garlic cloves, crushed
4 tablespoons lemon juice
1 cup sour cream
2 cups homemade mayonnaise (p. 183)
Salt and pepper
2 tablespoons gelatin
4 tablespoons water
3 egg whites
Mint leaves

Peel and pit avocados, and purée in a food processor or by pressing through a strainer. Turn into a bowl and stir in grated onion, chopped egg and crushed garlic. Mix lemon juice, sour cream and mayonnaise, beat into avocado mixture, season. In a bowl, sprinkle gelatin over water. Leave a moment, then heat over a pot of hot water until the gelatin dissolves. Pour into avocado mixture in a steady stream, beating all the time. Whisk egg whites until stiff and fold into mixture. Spoon into bowls of 1-cup capacity. Cover with plastic wrap and refrigerate for 3 hours. Serve garnished with mint leaves. Serves 12.

CHEESE & EGG STARTERS

BEET-PICKLED EGGS

Ingredients

2 beets, cooked and sliced
2 cups beet juice (left over from cooking)
2 cups red wine vinegar
1 tablespoon mixed pickling spices
12 hard-cooked eggs, shelled

Add sliced beets to the cooking juice, vinegar and pickling spices in a large pan. Bring to a boil, then remove from the heat. Place the eggs in a suitable container, pour the hot juice mixture over them and allow to cool. Refrigerate for 2 days or until eggs are beautifully red and have a sharp, zesty taste.

YOGURT CHEESE BALLS IN OLIVE OIL & HERBS

Ingredients

2 1/2 quarts plain yogurt
2 teaspoons salt
Finely chopped mint
Finely chopped marjoram

Finely chopped tarragon
Paprika
Olive oil

Line 2 strainers with scalded cheesecloth and place over bowls. Whisk salt into yogurt and pour into strainers. Drain overnight to become a creamy curd. Mold this into small rounds, place on a perforated dish and leave in refrigerator for 24 hours. Eat straight away, sprinkled with chopped herbs on slices of tomato. To keep, leave in refrigerator for 2-4 days, depending on how creamy you want them to be, then pack them into jars and cover with olive oil; store in a cool place.

Yogurt cheese balls in olive oil and herbs, served on thick slices of fresh tomato, alongside your own home-marinated olives (p. 201).

MEAT STARTERS

COOK'S NOTES:
To keep meatballs
from sticking to your
hands, simply moisten
your hands before you
mold each meatball.
Hey presto!

SPICED MEATBALLS WITH PEANUT DIP

Ingredients

1 pound ground lean beef
2 tablespoons plain yogurt
2 tablespoons soy sauce
1 teaspoon ground coriander
1 teaspoon ground turmeric
1 teaspoon olive oil
Salt and pepper
Vegetable oil for deep frying

For the Dip:
2 cups coconut cream
1/4 cup crunchy peanut butter
2 tablespoons dark brown sugar
1 teaspoon chili sauce
Salt and pepper

TO PREPARE THE DIP.
Place coconut cream in a saucepan and heat until quite hot but not boiling. Add peanut butter, sugar and chili sauce, and season to taste. Lower heat and stir gently until well combined. Remove from heat and set aside.

TO MAKE THE MEATBALLS.
Put the beef, yogurt, soy sauce, spices and olive oil into a bowl and season to taste. Squeeze the mixture together with your hands until it is well consolidated and clings together. Mold the mixture into about 50 bite-sized balls by rolling heaped teaspoonfuls in the palms of your hands.

Heat the vegetable oil in a frying kettle to 375°F. Deep-fry the meatballs, about 10 at a time, for 1-2 minutes only, until light brown in color. Remove with a slotted spoon and drain on paper towels.

To serve, reheat the dip and spear each meatball with a toothpick. Put the dip in a small bowl in the middle of a dish and surround with meatballs. Makes about 50.

CRISPY CHICKEN PIECES

Ingredients

2 pounds boneless chicken breasts,
*   skinned*
5 tablespoons soy sauce
2 tablespoons ground ginger
1 teaspoon dry mustard
6 tablespoons flour
3 eggs, beaten
2 cups white breadcrumbs
1/2 cup sesame seeds
Vegetable oil for deep frying

Cut chicken into about 100 thin, bite-sized strips. Put them into a large shallow dish and mix well with soy sauce, ginger and mustard.

Cover and leave to marinate for 1 hour. Coat the chicken strips in flour, dip into beaten egg, then coat with a mixture of the bread crumbs and sesame seeds. Squeeze into small sausage shapes. Arrange separately on small baking sheets and chill for a further 1-2 hours until firm.

Heat the oil in a skillet to 375°F. Cook about 12 pieces at a time for 5 minutes, turning frequently until golden-brown. Drain on paper towels and keep warm in oven while the remainder of the chicken pieces are cooked. Serve hot. Makes about 100.

PATÉ MAISON

Ingredients

1 cup mixed raw chicken and veal
1 garlic clove, cut in half
1 shallot, cut in half
3 slices raw bacon, chopped
6 slices prosciutto, chopped
1 egg
1 tablespoon brandy
A pinch each of salt, pepper & cinnamon
3 bay leaves

Pâté Maison. As well as being a substantial starter, this pâté could well be the gourmet treat of any picnic.

In a blender, food grinder or processor (using the steel knife blade), mix the chicken, veal, garlic and shallot until fine. Add the remaining ingredients except the bay leaves and grind everything until the mixture is smooth and finely chopped. Place in a 2-cup tureen with the bay leaves on top and bake in a preheated oven at 400°F for 40 minutes or until the pâté pulls away from the sides and is brown on top.

Cover and refrigerate when cold. Serve with crusty French bread.

Minty meat samosas . Preparing samosas can be a little time-consuming but not difficult. The availability of a pasta machine, however, makes the whole process effortless.

MINTY MEAT SAMOSAS

For the Dough:
3 cups flour
1/4 teaspoon salt
7 tablespoons ghee or clarified butter
2/3 cup cold water
A bunch of mint leaves
1/4 cup milk
Vegetable oil for frying

For the Filling:
3 tablespoons vegetable oil
1 tablespoon finely chopped ginger root
2 1/2 teaspoons finely chopped garlic
1 small onion, finely chopped
1 pound ground lamb
1/4 teaspoon cayenne
1 teaspoon salt
2 tablespoons hot water
1 tablespoon curry powder
1 teaspoon garam masala
1 teaspoon turmeric
1 tablespoon fresh lime juice

TO MAKE THE DOUGH.
Place the flour, salt and ghee into a bowl. Rub the ingredients together until they resemble bread crumbs. Add the water gradually (you may not need all of it) and

knead well for about 10 minutes. Cover the dough and leave to rest for an hour at room temperature.

When required, roll out the dough until quite thin, about 1/16-inch thick. Arrange the mint leaves on top of half the dough mixture in a regular pattern about 3/4-inch apart, then fold the other half of the rolled dough back on top so that the mint leaves are encased. Roll out the dough again into a very thin sheet.

The mint leaves should show through as a very decorative pattern. Cut into 3-inch squares or rounds. Place a teaspoon of filling in the center of each, brush the edges with milk and fold in half. Press the edges firmly together to seal in the filling. Deep-fry in oil until golden-brown.

TO MAKE THE FILLING.
Heat the oil and add the ginger, garlic and onion. Cook until the onion is soft and brown, then stir in the lamb. Add the remaining ingredients and cook over a low heat until most of the liquid has evaporated. Cool before use.

CHICKEN LIVERS & MUSHROOMS

Ingredients
18 chicken livers
1/2 cup mushrooms, sliced
4 tablespoons butter or margarine
1 tablespoon green sweet pepper,
        finely chopped
1 tablespoon parsley, chopped
1 tablespoon onion, finely chopped
1 tablespoon flour
1/2 cup dry white wine
1/2 cup chicken stock (p. 181)
1 bay leaf
1 teaspoon thyme
Salt and pepper
1 teaspoon nutmeg, grated

Sauté the livers and the mushrooms in the butter over a low heat for 3 minutes. Add the sweet peppers, parsley and onion. Cook for another 3 minutes, stirring frequently. Sprinkle flour over and when it is browned, gradually add white wine, chicken stock, bay leaf and thyme and simmer gently for a further 12 minutes. Stir from time to time, then season with salt and pepper and the nutmeg. Serve on toast. Serves 6.

SEAFOOD STARTERS

MUSSELS AU GRATIN

Ingredients
3 pounds mussels
1/4 cup dry white wine
1 very small onion, finely chopped
1/8 teaspoon vinegar
1/2 cup chopped parsley
2 garlic cloves, chopped
2/3 cup soft breadcrumbs
Salt and pepper
3 tablespoons oil
1 tablespoon lemon juice or vinegar

Wash, scrape beards off mussels. Discard
open ones, place the rest in a large, deep
pot with white wine, onion, pepper and
vinegar. Cover pot and cook over a high heat
until mussels open. Discard any that do not.
Drain, remove empty shell halves, keeping
those with mussel attached. Arrange them in
an ovenproof dish and cover with a mixture
of parsley, garlic and breadcrumbs, season to
taste. Combine oil and lemon juice, spoon
over mussels. Place in hot oven 425°F for a
few minutes and serve immediately. Serves 4.

TARAMASALATA

Ingredients
1/4 pound smoked cod's roe
1 slice stale bread, 2-inches thick
1 tablespoon grated onion (optional)
1 boiled floury potato
1 cup oil
Juice of 2 lemons
1/4 teaspoon paprika

Clean the roe by scraping away any loose
skin, then soak in water to remove some
of the salt. Remove crusts from the bread,
dip the rest into water and squeeze dry.
Blend onion to a fine pulp in a food
processor, then add the fish roe and blend
once more.

Next add the boiled potato and bread and
continue to mix until a smooth consistency
is obtained. Gradually add the oil and lemon
juice alternately until the color is a very pale
pink. The texture should be light and fluffy.
Season with the paprika and turn out into a
bowl. Serve with warm pita or crusty French
bread. Serves 6-8.

PARTY DIPS

PROVENCAL ANCHOVY DIP

Ingredients
6-8 canned anchovy fillets, drained
1 garlic clove, roughly chopped
3 tablespoons oil
1 teaspoon lemon juice
1/4 cup homemade mayonnaise (p 183)
1/4 cup light cream
1/4 teaspoon pepper
1/2 teaspoon paprika

Place the anchovy fillets and garlic in a bowl or mortar and grind to a pulp.

Add the oil, lemon juice, mayonnaise and the cream, mix well then season to taste with pepper.

Transfer to a decorative serving bowl and sprinkle with paprika.

Chill until ready to serve.

A DIP TO END ALL DIPS

Ingredients
2 cups sour cream
1 1/2 tablespoons grated horseradish
1 tablespoon paprika
1 tablespoon finely chopped chives
2 teaspoons tarragon
1 garlic clove, crushed
1/2 teaspoon salt
Pepper

Mix all the ingredients and chill thoroughly. Serve with a cold platter of mixed vegetables such as celery, carrot sticks and radishes.

Provençal anchovy dip. The strong flavors of anchovies and garlic combine in this dish to make an accompaniment to blander things, such as a raw vegetable platter.

COOKING
FOR
PARTIES

PREPARING FOR THE FUN

Whether you are cooking for two people or fifty, preparing for a party should be fun. That is why these delicious recipes are presented with straightforward instructions. The recipes serve from four to twenty people. Many of them may be doubled successfully — just remember that you should use less than twice the recommended liquid when you double the other ingredients. On the other hand, if you are halving a recipe, use more than half the recommended quantity of the liquid specified.

Parties range from intimate dinners for two or four, to cocktail parties, to buffet-style meals for a large crowd. So you will find a variety of recipes here, from finger food to roasts, and from brandy snaps to trifle. Whatever kind of party you organize, the key to success is in the planning. Will the guests be seated while they eat? How will the food be carried and served? Should food be cold or hot? Answers to these practical questions will help you choose a menu that suits the place as well as the occasion.

Many of these recipes can be prepared ahead. Some may be served cold, others need to be reheated but whichever you choose, they should be a great success.

Remember to read the recipe carefully and make a complete shopping list. You should also check to see that you have suitable cooking pans and serving dishes to cope with the ingredients. Perhaps you could borrow some extra serving platters from a good friend or neighbor, and return the favor on another occasion.

If your party is to be held out-of-doors, it is best to choose dishes that are easy to serve. If you have a distance to travel, you will need to be sure to keep some dishes cool while you are transporting them— egg custard and mayonnaise, for instance, should not be allowed to warm up.

Note: Fresh ginger root is used unless otherwise stated. Use fresh chilies or half the quantity of dried. It is preferable to use cold-pressed virgin olive oil but any type may be used. Vinegar is white wine fermented vinegar.

Trout and white wine is a perfect dish for a dinner party as you can prepare it in advance.

COOKING STARTERS

Whether you call these dishes hors d'oeuvres, starters, appetizers, or entrées, they can be used for many occasions–light lunches, cocktail parties or as a first course for a dinner party. Just remember, however, that starters should whet the appetite, not saturate it, and should harmonize with the main course that follows. When serving food at a cocktail party, be sure to present it attractively and at the correct temperature either chilled or piping hot.

SANDWICHES

Dainty sandwiches that can be eaten in two or three bites are appropriate to serve with drinks. They can be made in advance and you can choose such delicious fillings as thinly cut ham, turkey roll, smoked salmon, and cream cheese with herbs. You can ask your deli to slice the bread thinly or, if that is not possible, firm the uncut loaf in the freezer for an hour and cut it with a proper bread saw or a very sharp knife. The important point when making sandwiches is to organize the fillings. Whip the butter, have ready foil or waxed paper to wrap the sandwiches and plastic bags or boxes to store them in the refrigerator. Sandwiches will keep in excellent condition for up to 24 hours if wrapped in the following way.

Stack the filled sandwiches in bundles of three, place an outside lettuce leaf on top then cover closely in plastic wrap. When you have made six packages, place them in plastic boxes or bags for preference and store in the refrigerator or a cool room. When ready to serve, trim the crusts and cut into fingers or triangles.

CUCUMBER SANDWICHES

Small, perfect cucumber sandwiches are the ideal accompaniment to iced tea on the patio. Like tomato sandwiches, they are best assembled just before serving, but you can have the butter whipped, the cucumber sliced and salted, and the lettuce crisping in the refrigerator in advance. To prepare the cucumber, peel and slice it thinly, place on a flat plate, sprinkle with a teaspoon of salt, and leave to stand for 30 minutes. Drain and sprinkle with a few drops of vinegar. Place between thin slices of buttered white bread with finely shredded lettuce and season with pepper. Trim and cut with a good, sharp, serrated bread knife, and serve.

ASPARAGUS BOATS

Ingredients
For the Cheese Dough:
1/2 cup butter
1 1/2 cups flour
2 cups rat-trap cheese, grated
A pinch of salt
A dash of cayenne
2 tablespoons cold water

For the Filling:
2 tablespoons butter
3 slices streaky bacon, diced
3 scallions, chopped
1 cup light cream
3 tablespoons grated Parmesan cheese
3 eggs, beaten
Salt and pepper
1 1/2 pounds canned asparagus tips

Cream the butter and mix well with the other dough ingredients. Form into a ball, cover in plastic wrap and leave it in the refrigerator for at least 1 hour.

Roll out the dough thinly on a lightly floured board. Grease 12 molds with butter. Arrange close together. Lift the sheet of dough on a rolling pin and place loosely over the molds. Roll a small piece of dough into a ball and dip in flour. Use this to press the dough into the mold, then roll a well-floured rolling pin over the top

Cucumber sandwiches in preparation for a summer tea party.

COOK'S NOTES:
The best method to prevent bacon slices sticking to the pan is to start cooking the slices on a cold surface and bring the heat up gently.

(one way, then the other) to remove surplus dough. Roll out the trimmings again and use to line the remaining molds.

Melt butter and fry the bacon and scallions until the bacon is beginning to crisp. Add the cream and heat only until bubbles form; do not allow to boil. Remove from the heat, stir in the cheese, then the eggs, and season with salt and pepper.

Drain the asparagus and place a few tips in each dough shell.

Arrange the molds on a baking sheet and carefully pour in the filling to almost the top of the molds. Bake in a preheated moderate oven (350°F) for 15-20 minutes, or until the filling is puffed and golden brown and a knife inserted in the center comes out clean.

Serve warm or cold on the hors d'oeuvre tray. Makes 12-14.

MINTED CITRUS COCKTAIL

Ingredients
5 cups grapefruit segments
1 cup canned mandarin segments
1/2 cup orange juice
1/2 teaspoon Angostura bitters
1 tablespoon sherry
Sprigs of mint
8 maraschino cherries

Drain the grapefruit and mandarin segments and turn into a large bowl or jar. Add the orange juice, bitters and sherry and mix gently. Chill overnight.

Spoon the fruit cocktail into small, iced glass dishes. Decorate with mint sprigs and maraschino cherries. Serves 8.

DEVILS ON HORSEBACK

Ingredients
20 large prunes, pitted
20 whole blanched almonds
7 slices bacon

Stuff the prunes with the almonds. Stretch the bacon with the back of a knife, then cut each slice in three. Wrap each prune in a piece of bacon and secure with a wooden toothpick. Broil for 4-5 minutes on each side, until the bacon is crisp, or cook on a crumpled paper towel in a microwave oven for 3-4 minutes. Makes 20.

COCKTAIL MEATBALLS

Ingredients
2 pounds lean ground beef
1 pound sausage meat
2 large potatoes
1 medium-sized Granny Smith apple
2 large onions
2 slices bacon
2 eggs
2 teaspoons curry powder
1 teaspoon ground ginger
2 teaspoons superfine sugar
1/4 teaspoon dry mustard
Salt and pepper
1 tablespoon tomato ketchup
Flour for coating
Oil for frying

Peel and dice potatoes and apple. Finely chop onion. Place in a saucepan and just cover with water. Bring to a boil, then reduce heat and simmer until tender. Rub through a strainer, then mash and allow to cool

Chop the bacon finely and lightly beat eggs. Place all ingredients in a bowl and mix well together.

Using all-purpose flour, roll into bite-sized balls (place a little flour in a cup, add a small spoonful of mixture and quickly roll into a ball).

Heat a little oil in a skillet and fry the meatballs until golden brown. Drain on paper towels and serve hot or cold. The meatballs can also be baked in a moderately hot oven (375°F) for 15-20 minutes or until golden Makes about 100.

This recipe makes a large quantity of cocktail meatballs, a tasty offering to serve at the beginning of a party.

COOKS NOTES:
To make croûtes, remove crusts from three thick slices of stale bread. Cut each slice into four triangles and fry in 1 inch of hot oil. When golden, remove, sprinkle with salt and keep warm in the oven.

OYSTERS ROCKEFELLER

Ingredients
24 oysters on the shell
3/4 cup sour cream
2 garlic cloves, crushed with a little salt
Pepper
1 cup cooked spinach, finely chopped
6 tablespoons fine white breadcrumbs
2 tablespoons grated rat-trap cheese
2 tablespoons butter

Remove the oysters from their shells. Mix half the sour cream with half the crushed garlic and season with pepper. Place a teaspoon of the mixture in the bottom of each shell and place the oyster back in the shell.

Combine the spinach with the remaining sour cream and garlic, season with pepper and place a tablespoon of this mixture on each oyster.

Sprinkle with the bread crumbs and cheese. Arrange the oysters on rock salt in an ovenproof dish and place a small piece of butter on each. Place under a preheated broiler for about 4 minutes or until the breadcrumbs are a golden brown. Serve hot. Serves 4.

MUSHROOMS CORIANDER

Ingredients
2 pounds small white mushrooms,
*   quartered or whole*
1/3 cup lemon juice
4 teaspoons coriander seeds
1/3 cup olive oil
3 bay leaves
Salt and pepper

Clean the mushrooms with a cloth dipped in water and lemon juice. Trim the stalks. Cut the mushrooms into quarters and squeeze some lemon juice over them. Crush the coriander seeds in a mortar or with a rolling pin. Heat the olive oil in a heavy skillet over a low heat. Add the coriander seeds and allow to heat through. Add the mushrooms and bay leaves. Season with salt and pepper. Cook for 1 minute. Cover the skillet and allow the mushrooms to cook for a further 5 minutes over a very low heat, then leave to cool. Place the mushrooms in a dish and store in the refrigerator until required. Serves 8.

CILANTRO SOUP

Ingredients

1 cup chopped celery
1 cup chopped onion
2 teaspoons grated ginger root
1 garlic clove, crushed
1 tablespoon butter
1 tablespoon olive oil
1 tablespoon flour
1 1/4 quarts chicken stock, heated
1 cup fresh cilantro leaves
Salt and pepper
1 cup sour cream
Lemon juice
A few extra cilantro leaves

Heat butter and oil in a heavy-based saucepan and slowly cook the celery, onion, ginger root and garlic until soft. Sprinkle the softened vegetables with flour, slowly add the heated stock, bring to a boil, then reduce heat and simmer for 10 minutes. Remove from heat and stir in the cilantro leaves. Leave to stand for 10 minutes then purée in the food processor.

If serving hot, reheat, then stir in the sour cream and lemon juice. Garnish each portion with cilantro leaves. If serving chilled, refrigerate overnight. Serves 6.

Fresh cilantro soup to serve as a starter for a summer lunch or dinner.

MELON & HAM

Ingredients

1 large honeydew melon
3 ounces prosciutto
1 lemon

Slice the melon into crescents and remove seeds, fiber and rind. Wrap each crescent in wafer-thin slices of prosciutto and garnish each serving with half a slice of lemon. Serves 8.

SEAFOOD TEMPTATIONS

Baked buttered mussels make delicious finger food to hand around at a party. Be sure to serve them with plenty of small paper napkins.

JAPANESE SALMON SALAD

Ingredients
1 pound fresh salmon fillets
4 small avocados
3 teaspoons lemon juice
2 teaspoons wasabi
3 tablespoons light soy sauce
Shredded nori seaweed
Bean sprouts

Remove skin from the salmon and cut the flesh into small cubes. Halve avocados, remove the stones and peel. Cut into small cubes and toss gently in lemon juice to prevent discoloring.

Blend the wasabi with a little water to make a paste, then mix in the soy sauce. Toast the nori over a flame or under the broiler and use scissors to cut into thin strips. Just before serving, add the soy dressing to the salmon and avocado cubes and toss lightly. Arrange bean sprouts on individual plates and mound the salad on top. Sprinkle salads with the toasted nori strips and bean sprouts. Serves 8.

BAKED BUTTERED MUSSELS

Ingredients
1 tablespoon oil
4 dozen mussels, cleaned
1/4 cup butter
1/4 teaspoon garlic salt (optional)

Rub a large baking dish with oil and arrange mussels in a single layer. Place in hot oven (450°F) for 5-10 minutes, until the shells open. Do not over cook. Remove upper shells. Melt butter, add garlic salt. Serve mussels on the lower shells with a little butter and any liquid that has escaped into the pan poured over. Serves 4.

TROUT IN WHITE WINE

Ingredients

8 small to medium-sized trout
Salt and pepper
4 tablespoons chopped herbs
            (parsley, thyme and a little sage)
2 teaspoons grated lemon rind
1 tablespoon butter
1 1/2 cups chablis or other white wine
1 tablespoon butter and flour, blended
1 tablespoon tomato paste
1 cup light cream

Wash, dry and season trout. Place the fish in a buttered ovenproof dish. Sprinkle with the chopped herbs and lemon rind. Pour the wine around the fish and dot with knobs of butter. Cover with a piece of waxed paper and cook in a moderate oven (350°F) for 15-20 minutes.

Drain the trout and arrange on a warm serving dish. Keep hot. Strain the liquor from the fish into a small pan. Whisk in the blended butter, flour and the tomato paste, pour in the cream and cook for 2-3 minutes, stirring frequently.

Finally, coat the fish carefully with this sauce. Serves 8.

Oysters Kilpatrick are delicious because the oysters retain their essential flavor. Chop the bacon as finely as possible for the best result.

OYSTERS KILPATRICK

Ingredients

2 dozen oysters on the half shell
2 teaspoons Worcestershire sauce
2 tablespoons butter
2 slices bacon, finely chopped
Pepper

Arrange the oysters in a broiler. Heat the sauce and butter then spoon over the oysters. Sprinkle each oyster with finely chopped bacon and place under a heated broiler for 3 minutes or until the oysters are plump and the bacon crisp. Season with pepper and serve immediately. Serves 4.

Be sure to discard all the bones and skin when removing salmon from the can.

SALMON MOUSSE

Ingredients

Half a cucumber
2 tablespoons French dressing
3 teaspoons gelatin
3 tablespoons boiling water
1 8-ounce can salmon
1 tablespoon mayonnaise
2/3 cup heavy cream, chilled and whipped
Salt and pepper
A few drops of red food coloring (optional)
Lettuce pieces, tomato and lemon slices

Dice half of cucumber and steep in French dressing. Peel remaining cucumber and cut into slices. Boil for 5 minutes in salted water and drain. Dissolve gelatin in boiling water. Put salmon, including juice, boiled cucumber, mayonnaise, dissolved gelatin, with salt and pepper into a blender and blend until smooth. Season and add coloring. Blend until combined. Add diced cucumber, and fold in cream. Wet mold and pour in salmon mixture. Chill until set. Turn out onto a dish and garnish. Serve with horseradish sauce. Serves 4.

MARINATED TUNA FISH

Ingredients

4 fresh tuna cutlets

For the Marinade:
Juice of 1 orange
1/4 cup soy sauce
2 tablespoons chopped parsley
1 tablespoon lemon juice
1 garlic clove, crushed
1 teaspoon garam masala

Mix orange juice, soy sauce, parsley, lemon juice, garlic and garam masala. Place tuna in marinade and allow to stand for 3 hours. Remove tuna from marinade and place in a skillet. Baste with remaining marinade and cook for 4 minutes per side. Serve with green salad tossed in lemon juice. Serves 4.

MEAT DISHES

STUFFED PORK ROAST

Ingredients
2 1/2 pound piece of pork belly

For the Stuffing:
8 ounces pork-and-veal mince
8 ounces fresh breadcrumbs
1 medium-sized onion, finely chopped
1 egg, beaten
1 tablespoon chopped parsley
1/2 teaspoon ground sage,
*   oregano or rosemary*
Salt and pepper

Ask the butcher to remove bones and score the rind. Rub skin with oil, salt and leave to rest overnight in the refrigerator.

With a knife, make a shallow incision down the center of the belly meat, cutting towards but not through to the rind, and make two pockets. Combine the stuffing ingredients and place in the pockets in the meat. Roll the meat so that the two long ends meet around the stuffing, tie firmly at 1-inch intervals. Give the rind a second rubbing with salt and place on a rack in an open roaster. (This is important if you want every square inch of crust, as the rind will never become crisp at the point of contact with the baking dish.)

Bake in a preheated very hot oven (450°F) for 30 minutes, then reduce to 375°F for a further 1 1/4 hours. Potatoes may be baked around the meat. Remove to a warmed serving dish. Pour off excess fat and make gravy. If you like, stir in 1 tablespoon of marmalade. Serves 8.

Roast stuffed pork looks spectacular and is a surprisingly inexpensive dish to make.

SAUERBRATEN

Ingredients

3 pounds shin beef
2 cups vinegar or wine
2 cups water
2 onions, sliced
2 bay leaves
2 teaspoons salt
1 teaspoon black peppercorns
1 garlic clove, crushed
1/4 cup soft brown sugar or honey
Flour
2 tablespoons oil or drippings
2/3 cup sour cream

Cut beef into 1/2-inch slices and place in a heatproof dish. Prepare a marinade by combining vinegar or wine, water, onions, bay leaves, salt, peppercorns, garlic and sugar or honey. Heat gently but do not allow to boil. Pour the hot marinade over the meat, cover and when cool, store in refrigerator for 4-8 days. Turn meat each day. When ready to cook, drain the meat and set the marinade aside.

Pat the meat dry and roll in seasoned flour. Brown the meat in oil or dripping, add sliced onions, if desired, and half the marinade. Simmer gently for 1 1/2 hours, adding more marinade if necessary. Just before serving, season with salt and thicken gravy: combine 2 tablespoons flour with 1/2 cup cold water or marinade, add to the sauerbraten, bring to a boil and cook gently for a few minutes.

Add the sour cream to the thickened gravy but do not allow the cream to boil. Serve with boiled or mashed potatoes. Serves 8.

GALANTINE OF VEAL

Ingredients

5 pounds boneless veal, loin or shoulder
1 tablespoon butter
2 onions, sliced
2 carrots, sliced
1 cup beef stock
1 cup dry white wine
1 bay leaf
1 stalk celery
Sprig of thyme
Salt and pepper

For the Pork-and-Veal Stuffing:
1 tablespoon butter
2 scallions, chopped
4 ounces ham steak, diced

1 pound ground veal
1 pound ground pork
1 tablespoon pine nuts
2 tablespoons stuffed olives, sliced
1 tablespoon chopped parsley
2 eggs, lightly beaten
Salt and pepper

To make pork-and-veal stuffing, melt the butter, add the scallions and cook for 2-3 minutes. Place in a large mixing bowl, add all the other ingredients and mix well. Remove any excess fat and gristle from the veal and lay it out flat. Spread with pork-and-veal stuffing. Form a neat roll and sew up with strong thread or tie with string.

To prepare the meat, melt the butter in an open roaster and lightly brown the roll on all sides. Remove. Add the onions and carrots and cook for a few minutes. Lay the browned meat on top and pour over stock and wine. Add bay leaf, celery, thyme and seasoning. Cover and bake in a moderate oven 350°F for 2 1/2 hours, basting occasionally. Test with a skewer. If the juices that run out are clear, the meat is cooked. Remove the meat from the oven, and cool.

Strain stock and, when cold, remove the fat. Boil the stock rapidly to reduce to a syrupy consistency. Cool slightly. Untie the meat, brush with glaze.

Chill until ready to serve. Slice the meat and garnish with some sliced tomatoes, cucumbers and shredded lettuce or watercress. Serves 8-10.

VITELLO TONNATO

Ingredients
3 pound piece boneless veal fillet
2 anchovy fillets, cut into small pieces
1 tablespoon olive oil
1/3 cup dry vermouth
Salt and pepper
A bouquet garni
1 14-ounce can artichoke hearts

A wonderful addition to the buffet table. Guests will always welcome this aromatic galantine of veal when it is served.

For the Sauce:
6 ounces canned tuna
6 anchovy fillets
1 teaspoon capers
2 tablespoons lemon juice
1 tablespoon tomato paste (optional)
Salt and pepper
1/2 cup mayonnaise

Make some incisions in the surface of the meat with a sharp pointed knife and insert anchovy pieces. Roll up and tie neatly.

Heat the oil in a heavy casserole, preferably one into which the meat fits snugly, and brown the meat all over. Pour over the vermouth, season with salt and pepper then add the bouquet garni. Cover the casserole and cook in a moderate oven (350°F) for 1-1 1/4 hours.

Remove from the oven and allow veal to cool in the liquid, lift veal out and chill in the refrigerator to make the meat easier to carve.

To make the sauce, pound the tuna, anchovy fillets, capers, lemon juice and tomato paste (or process them in a blender) until smooth. Season with salt and pepper. Stir in the mayonnaise and then process in a blender or rub through a strainer.

Cut veal into thick, even slices, spread each slice with the sauce and reshape the joint. Leave in refrigerator until firm. Serve surrounded by artichoke hearts which have been rinsed, drained and tossed in vinaigrette dressing. Alternatively, the veal may be cut into thin slices, arranged on a platter, then covered with the sauce and served with lemon wedges and a dish of capers. Serves 8.

ENDIVE & HAM GRATIN

Ingredients

8 endive heads
3 tablespoons lemon juice
1/2 cup chicken stock
1/2 teaspoon salt
A pinch of superfine sugar
1 tablespoon butter
8 thin slices of ham
2 tablespoons grated cheese

For the Sauce:
1/4 cup butter
2 tablespoons flour
2 cups warm milk
Salt and pepper
2 tablespoons grated cheese

Remove outer leaves of endive and cross the base. Wash and drain. Place lemon juice, stock, salt, sugar and butter in a skillet and bring to a boil. Put endive on top, cover and simmer for 15 minutes. Turn vegetables and cook for 5 minutes.

Prepare sauce by melting butter in a pan, add flour, and stir. Cook on low heat for 1 minute, then slowly beat in warm milk until smooth. Simmer for 15 minutes. Drain and wrap a slice of ham round each endive. Place in a low-sided baking dish. Add liquid from skillet to sauce, stir, season and add half the grated cheese. Pour sauce over endive. Scatter cheese on top and place under a broiler to brown. Serves 8.

BAKED GLAZED HAM

Ingredients
A 14-pound cured ham on the bone
or a10-pound boneless ham

For the Glaze:
1 1/2 cups soft brown sugar
2 teaspoons dry mustard
1/2 cup clear honey
Whole cloves
1/2 cup orange juice

Cut a scallop pattern around the thick end of the ham shank and ease skin away from the fat. Turn ham over and ease away remaining skin. Place the ham, fat side uppermost, on a rack in a roasting pan containing 1 1/2-inches of water. Cover pan with foil, and bake in a preheated moderately slow oven (325°F) for 1 hour. Remove from oven and pour off liquid. Using a sharp knife, score fat with 1/4-inch deep diagonal cuts, first one way, then the other, to form a diamond pattern. Mix sugar, mustard and honey together and, using a brush, spread half the mixture over ham. Stud each diamond with a clove. Mix the remaining glaze with orange juice. Increase oven temperature to hot (400°F) and bake ham for a further 30-40 minutes, basting it every 10 minutes with remaining glaze. Serve hot or cold. Serves 20-25.

COOK'S NOTES:
Never discard left-over wine. You can use it for deglazing a roasting pan–red wine is especially good when making gravy. White wine is good for poaching fish. The bottles should be corked to keep wild yeasts at bay and they can be topped up with other wines.

COOK'S NOTES:
To carve a ham, first remove a slice from underneath, to allow the ham to sit flat. With a sharp knife, make a vertical cut approximately 4 inches from the knuckle. Make a second cut at an angle to the first and remove the wedge formed. Cut several thin slices right down to the bone, parallel to the second cut. Carve along the bone and remove slices.

CHICKEN DELIGHTS

ARROZ CON POLLO

Ingredients

2 2 1/2-pound chickens,
*   each cut into 6 pieces*
2 teaspoons dried oregano
1/2 teaspoon pepper
Salt
1/2 cup salad oil
2 cups onion, finely chopped
1 garlic clove, crushed
1 medium-sized green sweet pepper
1 bay leaf
1/4 teaspoon paprika
1 teaspoon saffron threads
2 cups long-grain rice
1 14-ounce can tomatoes
2 cups chicken stock
1/2 pound frozen green peas
1 red sweet pepper

Wash the chicken pieces and dry well.
Combine oregano, pepper and 2 teaspoons
salt. Sprinkle the mixture all over the
chicken. Rub in well. leave for 10 minutes.
In a large casserole, heat the oil over
medium heat. Brown the chicken a third at
a time until golden-brown all over. Remove
the chicken and keep warm. Cut green
pepper into lengthwise strips, 1/2-inch
wide. To the drippings in casserole, add
the onion, garlic, green sweet pepper, bay
leaf and paprika, and sauté, stirring, over
medium heat until the onion is tender.

Using the back of a spoon, crush the
saffron threads on a small piece of foil.
Add rice with 2 teaspoons salt to the
casserole. Cook, stirring, until rice is lightly
browned, about 10 minutes. Add the
undrained tomatoes and chicken stock.
Arrange chicken on the rice mixture. Bring
to a boil. Bake, covered, in a preheated
moderate oven (350°F) for 1 hour.

Remove from the oven and add 1/2 cup
water. Sprinkle peas over the top. Cut red
pepper into 1/2 inch strips and arrange
attractively over the top. Bake, covered,
for a further 20 minutes or until chicken
is tender, peas are cooked and rice has
absorbed all the liquid. Remove from oven
and leave to stand, covered, for 10 minutes.
Serve from the casserole. Serves 8.

OVEN-FRIED LEMON CHICKEN

Ingredients
2 2 1/2-pound chickens
1 cup flour
2 teaspoons salt
1/2 teaspoon pepper
1 tablespoon paprika
3/4 cup butter or margarine

For the Sauce:
1 tablespoon soy sauce
1 teaspoon pepper
1/2 cup oil
1/2 cup lemon juice
1 tablespoon grated lemon rind
2 garlic cloves, crushed

Combine all the sauce ingredients, mix well and refrigerate for 1 hour. Combine the flour, salt, pepper and paprika. Cut the chicken into serving sized pieces and toss in seasoned flour. Grease a large ovenproof dish. Arrange chicken pieces skin-side down in single layer. Melt butter, spoon over chicken, bake uncovered in a preheated hot oven (400°F) for 30 minutes. Turn chicken, spoon over lemon sauce and cook for a further 30 minutes or until tender, basting occasionally. Serves 8-12.

CIRCASSIAN CHICKEN

Ingredients
4 pounds chicken pieces
1 onion
1 carrot
A few sprigs of parsley
1 teaspoon salt
1/2 teaspoon pepper

For the Sauce:
2 cups walnut halves
3 slices white bread
1 cup chicken stock
1-2 tablespoons walnut oil
1 tablespoon paprika

Oven-fried lemon chicken is a succulent dish, perfect for entertaining. It can be made well in advance and just put in the oven when needed, leaving you plenty of time to talk to the guests.

Not only is Circassian chicken a delicious treat, it is actually good for you.

COOK'S NOTES:
Cayenne pepper is much stronger than black pepper. (In fact, it is so hot that it must be used in tiny pinches). But it is marvellous in sauces, smoked fish and cooked cheese dishes. Those who want a milder taste should use paprika, which is used in goulash and rice dishes and heightens the color of broiled or barbecued shellfish.

Place chicken, onion, carrot, parsley, salt and pepper in a pan and cover with water. Simmer very gently for 1 hour, or until chicken is tender. Leave covered to cool.

Remove skin and bones from chicken and cut pieces into strips and set aside in refrigerator while preparing the sauce. Finely blend walnuts and 1 slice of bread in a food processor. Break remaining bread into cubes and drop into blender while still running. Slowly add chicken stock through feed tube. When a smooth consistency, season with salt and pepper. Mix half the walnut paste with the chicken and place in serving dish. Cover with remaining paste. Just before serving, combine oil and paprika and dribble over the surface. Serve chilled. Serves 8.

A CHOICE OF SALADS

AVOCADO SALAD

Ingredients
2 ripe avocados
2 tomatoes, finely chopped
1 small onion, finely chopped
1 teaspoon paprika
1 teaspoon salt
1/2 teaspoon pepper
Juice of 1 lemon
1 romaine lettuce, thoroughly washed
1 tablespoon chopped parsley

Halve avocados, peel and cut into small pieces. In a deep bowl, mash the avocados, tomatoes and onion with the back of a large spoon. Add paprika, salt and pepper, pour on the lemon juice and stir well.

Line the bottom and sides of a salad bowl or a large plate with the romaine lettuce leaves.

Add avocado salad to the center of the bowl and garnish with the chopped parsley. Chill in the refrigerator for 30 minutes and serve. Serves 6-8.

Greek country salad is perfect for an outdoor summer lunch party. People have been enjoying this type of salad for hundreds of years.

GREEK COUNTRY SALAD

Ingredients
1 lettuce
A bunch of radishes
1 cucumber
4 tomatoes
1/2 cup black olives
1/2 pound fetta cheese

For the Dressing:
5 tablespoons olive oil
1 1/2 tablespoon vinegar
2 garlic cloves, crushed
2 tablespoons chopped mint
Salt and pepper

COOK'S NOTES:
It is advisable to snip chives finely just before you serve, as their flavor is best when freshly prepared. This is usually done with scissors directly over a bowl of green salad or scrambled eggs.

Wash the lettuce and crisp it in the refrigerator. Trim radishes, cut cucumber in thick slices and the tomatoes in wedges. Tear the lettuce into bite-sized pieces and place in bowl with prepared vegetables, black olives and fetta cheese cut into 1-inch cubes.

Combine the dressing ingredients, shake well and pour over the salad. Toss and serve immediately. Serves 8.

MUSHROOMS A LA GRECQUE

Ingredients

1 pound button mushrooms
1 tablespoon fresh tarragon
        or 1 teaspoon dried tarragon
1 tablespoon lemon juice
1 garlic clove
1 tablespoon finely chopped parsley
1 tomato, peeled, seeded and chopped
A pinch of thyme
Salt and pepper
1 bay leaf
1/4 cup olive oil
1 cup water

Carefully wipe the mushrooms, trim stems, and slice lengthwise. Place with remaining ingredients in a heavy saucepan. Cover and bring to a boil. Reduce the heat and cook gently until mushrooms are tender but firm, 8-10 minutes. Leave to cool, then chill. Serve with crusty rolls. Serves 6-8.

CURRIED CHICKEN & MANGO SALAD

Ingredients

2 chicken breasts, cut in halves
1 tablespoon lemon juice
2 mangoes, peeled and sliced
1 cup celery chopped
1/4 cup plain yogurt
1/4 cup mayonnaise
1 1/2 teaspoons curry powder
1/2 teaspoon ground cumin
3/4 cup roasted cashew nuts, chopped
2 tablespoons chopped cilantro leaves
Mixed salad greens, washed and crisp

Poach chicken breasts in salted water to cover for about 15 minutes, and allow to cool in a pan of stock. Remove skin and bones and cut chicken into bite-sized pieces. Combine the chicken, lemon juice, mangoes, celery and shallots. In a small bowl whisk together the yogurt, mayonnaise, curry powder and cumin. Add the dressing to the chicken mixture with salt and pepper to taste. Cover and chill for several hours.

Just before serving, stir in the cashews and cilantro. Serve on crisp salad greens. Serves 6.

SPINACH SALAD WITH YOGURT DRESSING

Ingredients
1/2 pound young spinach
3 ounces ricotta cheese
2 tablespoons yogurt
1 tablespoon wine vinegar
2 tablespoons chopped chives
1 tablespoon chopped parsley
Salt and pepper

Remove any stalks from the spinach, wash the leaves and gently pat dry with paper towels. Roll up leaves like a cigar and slice into 1-inch strips. In a large mixing bowl beat the cheese and yogurt until smooth, add the vinegar, chopped chives and parsley then season with salt and pepper. If dressing is too thick, add a more yogurt. When ready to serve, add the spinach to the dressing and toss the salad. Turn into a salad bowl and decorate with the flowers of chives or marigold petals. Serves 6.

Decorate the spinach salad with yogurt dressing and rosebuds.

JUST DESSERTS

SWEET SHERRY TRIFLE

Ingredients
1 jelly roll, cut into 1-inch slices
2 teaspoons gelatin
1/4 cup hot water
3/4 cup sweet sherry
3 eggs, separated
5 tablespoons superfine sugar
2 tablespoons lemon juice
3/4 cup heavy cream
Extra heavy cream for decorating

Make sweet sherry trifle with chocolate sponge roll for a change. It is easy to make and looks so special.

Brush a glass dish with sherry. Line dish with jelly roll slices. Dissolve gelatin in hot water add sherry. Cool, chill for 30 minutes until mixture thickens. Beat egg yolks until frothy, add 2 tablespoons sugar and beat until yolks are thick and lemony. Whip egg whites until frothy. Add sugar, beating constantly. Add the lemon juice and beat until the mixture is stiff but not dry. Add sherry and gelatin mixture into egg yolks and combine. Whip cream and fold in. Fold in egg whites thoroughly. Pour into lined glass dish. Chill until firm. Serves 8.

RICE TYROLHOF WITH APRICOT SAUCE

Ingredients
For the Rice:
1 cup short-grain rice
2 1/2 cups milk
2 eggs, separated
2 tablespoons superfine sugar
1 orange
2 teaspoons gelatin

1 dessert apple, diced
1 cup strawberries or grapes sliced
1 tablespoon finely chopped candied peel

For the Apricot Sauce:
1/2 cup apricot jam
1 tablespoon lemon juice
2 teaspoons lemon peel
3 tablespoons hot water

Combine all the sauce ingredients and chill. Simmer rice with milk until soft and creamy, 25-30 minutes. Remove from heat. Beat egg yolk with sugar and stir into the rice. Add 2 teaspoons grated orange peel and candied peel.

Dissolve gelatin in the orange juice over hot water and add to the rice with fruit. When cool, add beaten egg white and pour into a serving dish. Chill. Serve with apricot sauce. Serves 6.

ITALIAN REFRIGERATOR CAKE

Ingredients
1 cup flour
3/4 teaspoon baking powder
1/4 teaspoon salt
2 egg yolks
1/2 cup cold water
1 cup superfine sugar
1 teaspoon vanilla extract
1/2 teaspoon lemon extract
2 egg whites

For the Frosting:
1/3 cup chocolate chips
3/4 cup superfine sugar
1 pound ricotta cheese
1/2 teaspoon ground cloves
2 tablespoons grated lemon peel
2 tablespoons grated orange peel
2 tablespoons sweet vermouth

Sift flour, baking powder and salt together. Beat egg yolks and water until fluffy and treble in volume. Add sugar gradually and continue beating until light and thick. Stir in vanilla and lemon extract. Add the flour mixture all at once, folding it in with a rubber spatula. Whisk the egg whites until stiff peaks form, and fold into mixture.

Place in two greased and lined 8-inch sandwich tins and bake in a preheated moderate oven (350°F) for 20-25 minutes.

Invert the pans on wire racks and leave until they are cold. Remove the pans and lining paper. Melt the chocolate chips in a bowl over hot water. Stir in the sugar and

COOK'S NOTES:
Always choose a metal spoon in preference to a wooden spoon when folding in egg white. The job is easier if you first mix in a tablespoon of the beaten egg white before folding in the remainder.

vermouth and spread the frosting over the top and sides of cake using a palette knife. Chill for about 4 hours before serving. Serves 8.

CHAMPAGNE SORBET

Ingredients
1 1/2 cups water
1 cup granulated sugar
Grated peel of 2 lemons
Juice of 2 lemons
1 1/4 cups heavy cream
1 1/4 cups plain yogurt
1/4 bottle sweet champagne
1 egg white

Place the water, sugar with the lemon peel in a saucepan and simmer for 10 minutes. Cool and combine with the lemon juice. Lightly whip the cream, fold in yogurt and strain in cooled lemon juice and syrup.

Pour into a container and freeze until mushy. Remove from the freezer, beat well and then add the champagne. Freeze again to the mushy stage. Beat again and fold in the stiffly beaten egg white. Freeze until firm and serve with a sponge fingers or wafers. Serves 8.

You can use any extra champagne to top up the champagne sorbet, or drink it separately. Whichever way, it is bound to be a success.

remaining ingredients, except vermouth, and mix well. Chill in the refrigerator for 30 minutes before using. Put one cake layer onto a serving plate. Sprinkle with half the vermouth and spread with less than half the filling. Top with a second layer and sprinkle with the remaining

INDEX